Accepting NO Limits!

Soaring Above All Circumstances

Rikki L. Webber
International Travel Photographer

Copyright © 2017 Rikki Webber

Accepting NO Limits
SOARING ABOVE ALL CIRCUMSTANCES

Printed in the USA

ISBN (print): 978-0-9988355-0-1

ISBN (kindle): 978-0-9988355-1-8

Library of Congress Control Number: 2017904226

Published by L.I.P. by Rikki, LLC | New Albany, Ohio

All Rights Reserved. This book is protected by the copyright laws of the United States of America. This book may not be copied or reprinted for commercial gain or profit. The use of short quotations is permitted. Permission will be granted upon request. The author guarantees all contents are original and do not infringe upon the legal rights of any other person or work.

Scripture taken from the New King James Version of the Bible is marked NKJV. Copyright © 1982 by Thomas Nelson, Inc. Used by permission. All rights reserved.

To Contact the Author:

www.rikkilwebber.com

Dedication

This book is lovingly dedicated to:

The Glory of God my Heavenly Father

Who has shown me unconditional love by sending His only begotten Son to demonstrate this type of love for me. I am blessed and highly favored more than I could ask or imagine. The best is yet to come!

Alyssa

My miracle, my Baby Girl, my travel buddy, living a life of faith and prayer. Not a day goes by that I am not praying for your continued success. No matter what comes, keep holding God's hand and never let go, keep living the life of a courageous, bold woman of God that you are and believe by faith that dreams do come true. Without fail you continue to make me a very proud Mom! ~ Bambi

Roxanne

My Mom, whose support and love for me over the years has never failed to lift me out of a life of frustration and defeat. I will always be eternally grateful for the time you spent with Alyssa and I here in Ohio to participate in your first 5k and to make sure I had the time to pen this book. Your latter days will be greater!

My Loving Church Family

The Worship Center of Central Ohio, under the great leadership of Apostle David S. Carter. Words cannot express the gratitude that I have for each of you for your love and support for all that I do. May God bless you for always loving and accepting Alyssa and I as family.

Praise For Accepting No Limits!

Accepting No Limits! Soaring Above All Circumstances, is a message of honest reflection and resiliency. Rikki's willingness to share her personal journey is one that can uplift and inspire many. Too many times people feel alone in their life's journey-this is the book that will remind you-you are not alone, and with His Grace, you can be limitless!

SHIRELLE JACKSON
*ASSISTANT ATHLETIC DIRECTOR FOR
STUDENT ATHLETE DEVELOPMENT
UNIVERSITY OF MIAMI*

This book is a helpful compass that Rikki has placed in the hands of people who have a directional pull toward their purpose and assignment, but their surroundings don't match their vision. On each page you will find hope as she encourages you to never let what you see in the natural determine what your heart believes in the Spirit.

BISHOP EDWARD STEPHENS, JR.
*GOLDEN GATE CATHEDRAL
MEMPHIS, TN*

This literary work is a dynamic tool for those who are attempting to overcome their circumstance and attain what God has for them. The author employs her own spiritual formation and journey to lead the readers to a place of transformation, which eradicates the paradigm of life limitations. This work successfully aides in removing the systemic bondage that leads many to a life of underachievement. The implementation of this work into the daily lives of the readers will truly lead them to a life of no limits.

DR. JONATHAN J. MCREYNOLDS
PASTOR OF AENON MISSIONARY BAPTIST CHURCH
ROCHESTER, NEW YORK

IX	**Foreword**
1	**Chapter One** *A Spoken Word*
22	**Chapter Two** *The Early Years*
23	**Chapter Three** *Internal Reconstruction*
45	**Chapter Four** *Re-Alignment*
85	**Chapter Five** *Recovering*
105	**Chapter Six** *It's Not Just About You*
121	**Chapter Seven** *Ready to Soar*
121	**Appendix** *Travel Photo Gallery*

Accepting NO Limits

Foreword

Have you ever heard someone tell their life's story and the challenges and obstacles they had to face and overcome and said, "That sounds like a movie," or "you should write a book about that!" Well *"Accepting No Limits! Soaring Above All Circumstances"*, is one of those books.

First time author Rikki Webber chronicles a portion of her life's story from her upbringing as a child through her adult life where she went from a comfortable life and lifestyle, to losing it all, living in the basement of family friends, living in a car and having to start all over again. All the while as she faced these real life challenges, she did her best to shield her teenage daughter, Alyssa, and canine companion, Diamond, from the adversities they were experiencing and that she believed they would eventually overcome.

In the midst of the challenges, although the circumstance bleak, devastating and sometimes even humiliating, Rikki continued, with a dogged determination and persistence, that God would honor His Word and would deliver her from the pit to the palace.

Accepting No Limits will both challenge and encourage you that no matter where you find yourself in life, with faith, determination and action, your negative circumstances are not the ceiling but the floor.

It's a story of faith, hope, determination and a belief in the promises of God that will allow you to "Soar above all circumstances" and walk in the plans, purposes and destiny God has designed and determined for you.

As one who has served as her Pastor since 1999, and who licensed and ordained her into the ministry, Rikki's walk with the Lord has always been saturated by faith. She's the very one that would "speak those things that be not, as though they were," even if other's doubted her sanity. For Rikki, faith is not a noun but a verb and this work is the culmination of a life, lived by faith, walking by faith, speaking by faith and now, we have an opportunity to read what the facts that a life of faith will accomplish. With God, all things are possible. "Accepting No Limits" begin a life where you will "Soar Above all Circumstances!"

Rikki's first offering is a must read and an encouragement for wherever you find yourself in life.

Enjoy!

APOSTLE DAVID S. CARTER, M. DIV.
YALE DIVINITY SCHOOL
THE WORSHIP CENTER OF CENTRAL OHIO
COLUMBUS, OHIO
WCCOIMPACT.ORG

Chapter One
A Spoken Word

Wait: *Chakah*

"Now Joseph had a dream…"
- GENESIS 37:5 NKJV

"And so we have the prophetic word confirmed, which you do well to heed as a light that shines in a dark place, until the day dawns and the morning star rises in your hearts, knowing this first, that no prophecy of Scripture is of any private interpretation, for prophecy never came by the will of man, but holy men of God spoke as they were moved by the Holy Spirit."
- 2 PETER 1:19 -21 NJKV

How many times have we heard people say, "I'm not a writer, why would I write a book?" Or, "I'll wait until I reach the end of my journey to share my story with others to help someone else along who may be going through the same struggles that I've gone through."

That certainly was my perspective on writing a book. It was never a thought for me to write one, or to become a published author. I am an avid reader of fiction and non-fiction books. In fact one of my favorite past-times is reading. I enjoy books on leadership, empowerment, self-help, motivational, and photography.

I also love all of the "tear jerker" books where the characters win at the end. My favorite contemporary romance, literature and fiction author is Danielle Steel. I must own almost every book she has ever written. I was introduced to her books back when I was attending Bloomfield High School in Bloomfield, Connecticut. At that time a classmate and I were discussing books that we enjoyed reading and she introduced me to the writings of Danielle Steel. After purchasing one of her books I began reading it and I found that I could not put it down and I read through it that weekend, I was hooked.

Her books took me places that I've only dreamt I could go. I got lost in her characters as they rode the train in Europe or had Tapas in Spain. I was with them when they skied on the slopes of Aspen or walked the paths of the Grand Canyon. I learned so much from her books. Everything from how a lady should carry herself, to how the wealthy lived in the skyscrapers in Manhattan and even what it was like to have a limousine driver pick you up at the front door as the doorman held the elevator for you.

Yes, Danielle Steel is the one that I can thank for wanting to travel to the ends of the world and go to all the places that she took her readers through her characters in every book she's ever written. I hope to one day meet her face to face and to thank her for giving a girl like me, from the suburbs of Connecticut, a sense of adventure through her novels. To know that no matter what struggles you face in life that you can escape through a book, and one day it can become your reality. I have been a die-hard fan ever since.

With that type of writing and other non-fiction writings of authors past, present and future, never in a million years could I fathom that I would be one in that number. However, God had His plans for me.

Before we get to my present day life, I want to take you back some years so you can see that when God thought about our lives from the end to the beginning, He knew the journey we would take to get us to the place of being in His perfect will. At times He will show us our destiny, He allows us to "peep" into our future. He just doesn't reveal all the details of the journey, but allows us to walk it out, by faith, with Him as our Guide.

My daughter, along with her dog, Diamond, and I were living a very comfortable life in New Albany, Ohio—one of the top rated suburbs in Ohio three years in a row—in a 3-story condo. My daughter was going to a "blue ribbon" awarded public school, I was driving a Volvo with no cares for shoes, clothes, or food, and we were very comfortable.

Everything that I had then was not given to me. I didn't come from a family of wealth. We had very little means, but I never knew that until I was older. My parents always did their best to make sure we had shelter, food, and clothes. Pursuing a higher education upon finishing high school was always in the back of my mind.

College was never a conversation with my parents, perhaps because they didn't have the funds to send us. Never did they talk to us about finding other ways to finance this higher education. I'm going to assume that is because it was never in their realm of thinking as neither of them attended college either.

There were never any degrees hung on the walls in our homes (we were one of those families that moved every other year and not because we were military). A college degree has never hung on any wall in my home as an adult either; I have numerous certificates but not ONE college degree. Not because I didn't want one, but that was NOT part of God's plans for my life. Having a college degree was not my story.

However, this was not going to be an option for my daughter. At a very early age I planted that seed of attending college right out of high school. We weren't allowing any time for that ink to dry on her diploma, as that would allow a crack for doubt to set in.

I was accepted to colleges, I applied to community colleges, night school, you name it, and I applied to it. God would not open that door no matter how hard or how long I would knock. God had spoken to me some years ago during my young adult years, even when I was still applying for community college, because I felt it was important for me to have a college degree. He said, "You will not attend or graduate from any college. What I am going to do through you I do not want a higher institution getting the glory. All of the glory will go to Me." That word was given to me after years of trying to get into schools, well after I graduated high school.

Before getting that word from Him, He did allow me to go to a business school right out of high school. That was a nine-month course and then I wanted more. Though it wasn't His plans to allow me to attend other schools that business school helped me to sharpen my business skills that I still use to this very day. God's ways are not our ways. He knows what we need and will allow it, if we just adhere to His will. We can save ourselves so much time if we just listen to Him and acknowledge Him from the beginning. I have learned that a "no" from God is an answer.

Though a college degree wasn't in the plans, that didn't stop me from doing well in life. I am self-taught in so many areas in my life. I have a certificate for almost every class and/or course I've ever attended. I may even hold a record for the number of certificates I have.

At times we get so caught up in our own self and situations that we make consulting God a last resort. God wants to be a priority in our lives, not an after-thought. Until we grasp that concept He will undoubtedly bring us to "dead ends" until we reprioritize our way of processing our cares of this world.

> *"Therefore humble yourselves under the mighty hand of God, that He may exalt you in due time, casting all your cares on Him, for He cares for you."*
> ~ 1 PETER 5:6-7 NKJV

Though we were living a comfortable life and things were going well for us, that didn't prevent me from being laid off. I picked up odd jobs here and there and the feeling of comfort started slowly turning into anxiety. Being a single mom of a high school student, I wasn't sure what to do next but I knew I had to find work. Having had many spiritual encounters with God over the years, I was not surprised to have Him speak to my heart to give me divine direction for my situation at hand.

During a school break we took a trip to visit family in Connecticut. This was some time in 2006 around my 30s; I received a prophetic word that would turn my life, as I knew it upside down, for His glory.

During this trip, I went to spend my Sunday morning in worship at First Cathedral, as I normally would. This is where I accepted Christ at the age of 19.

I started that morning in one of the Sunday school classes. As I sat in the class I wasn't paying too close attention because I was worrying about my issues at hand.

These moments are distractions and could cause us to miss out on what is being taught. I was so distracted with my issues, my current life, like having been laid off from a full-time job and in the hunt for another, and in the meantime, I was working part-time and taking photos for friends and their weddings, or family pictures and not earning enough steady income. I was distracted by not knowing how I would get the work that I needed to make the income that I was making before getting laid off. Isn't that like us? Allowing distractions of any kind to interfere with us while in church?

As I sat through the lesson with a heavy heart and the distractions I was trying to "listen" for God to give me an answer or a sign, direction of some sort. Something that would help to clear my heart and mind. Then NOTHING, absolutely nothing.

Though class was ending and there was no answer from God it was time to prepare for the second service. I just knew I'd get my answers then. God always speaks to His children in service at some point, doesn't He? I was determined to take my thoughts captive so not to allow any distractions to make me miss God speaking to me!

Leaving the class to get ready for service, I politely stopped and spoke to other members that I saw while heading for a seat in the sanctuary. We exchanged hugs and kisses and fond memories while catching up.

As I turned to walk away my eyes went in the direction of this woman of God that was sitting in the same class that I was just in. She was no stranger to me. I knew her from my days of going to that church and it was great seeing her again.

Clear Direction

I walked over to her, we hugged and chatted a bit. As we were standing, exchanging pleasantries, she got into this "God has a word for you" stance. She began to pray and she translated the message that she just spoke to me in "tongues."

Tongues is a prayer language that God gives us. It is, praying and/or speaking in an unknown language to God while the Holy Spirit gives the interpretation. This was the prayer language she was using at that time. This language confuses the devil. I urge everyone that doesn't have this language to desire it of God.

It was clear that God was using her to speak directly into my life. It confirmed what I was living and currently seeking an answer and direction for. The words she spoke made a lasting impression, giving me the clear direction I needed at my current fork in the road. The words she spoke were, "He wants you to stop working every job except photography. He is going to use you and the photos that you take to bring the world to other people to see His creation. He is going to use you as His eyes and show you what to capture."

The words she spoke made a lasting impression, giving me the clear direction I needed.

God allowed such a strong, prophetic woman of God to speak this direction into my life. I am grateful for her obedience to speak the anointed word from God to me. It was the beginning of a new chapter in my life. This prophet of God had no idea what was going on in my life. How could she? We weren't in any similar circles; I live in Ohio and she in Connecticut. I wasn't using any form of social media at the time so she didn't have any knowledge of my circumstances through that resource either. I'm certain she's not a mind reader and read my thoughts while we were both in class. This was God through and through.

As tears were streaming down my face, all I could do was hug her as if I were hugging Him. I have my answer about my career now and I was grateful. She went on to tell me the kind of money I'll be making from the photos and other details that I will leave out of this book. The vision is yet for an appointed time. Just know that we don't serve a broke God. Hallelujah!

We chatted for a bit more and then I was off to find a seat in the sanctuary. I was excited about my divine destiny and contentment, that God spoke a word of direction to me that wonderful Sunday morning in 2006.

This word seemed simple enough. I was to do photography and nothing else. I loved photography and did it as a hobby. Now it would become my career. We shouldn't overlook the "oil" in our house (2 Kings 4:1-7). It's so important to us that we seek God for direction in our lives. He wants us to live off of the surplus. Not to be a slave to debt.

I was elated with this word because it spoke to what was my "hobby" at the time, but something I love and enjoy doing. I now have my direction; photography was no longer a hobby, but now my career. All the other odd jobs had to go.

What has God placed in you to use for His glory? If you are struggling with your career, seek God before you make any drastic changes. As you seek God, take a mental inventory of the "oil" that's in your "house." The passion He has designed in you should be your starting point.

The thing that I've come to learn about a prophetic word from God is that He has no time or date stamp on them. We don't know how long it will take for a prophetic word will come to pass or to manifest.

As with Joseph, it took over 20 years before it would manifest. While waiting for the manifestation, it is up to us to keep that word protected and to pray over it constantly until we are walking in it. We are a work in progress. Don't sit around waiting on the manifestation. "The thief (the devil) does not come except to steal, and to kill, and to destroy" John 10:10 NJKV, and that includes the prophetic word spoken to us.

What are you going to do to protect what God has given to you? I'm certainly not going to just hand it over to the enemy. Fight for it I must (spoken like the character, "Yoda" in Star Wars). It's mine, He spoke it to me, I will guard it and I will have faith to believe that I will see His promises spoken to me, this side of heaven.

When it was time to head back to Ohio, I had joy in my heart and determination on the brain. Now I have a spoken word from God to go along with my faith. Little did I know this was the beginning of a very long journey through the valley of dry places before I would reach my "promised land."

Hurry Up and Wait

When I returned to Ohio, I was on fire. I was on a mission. I tapped into my organizational gifts and put a game plan together. I had to prepare myself for the manifestation of God's promises. I was determined to see it come to pass and not sit idly by waiting on it. I believed this to be the start of a photography business. So instead of sitting by hoping for someone to come along and do it for me; I had to roll up my sleeves and start researching business startups.

So many times after we receive a prophetic word, we jump out of bed each day expecting. Remember that excitement the night before your birthday or Christmas Eve? It's that same type of excitement. I'd wake up every morning wondering is it today? Did God deliver on His promises today? And we wait, and wait, and wait. Then days turn into weeks, weeks into months, and months into years. And still nothing. Not a single sign of God doing what He said He was going to do. These are the times to pray against doubt and discouragement because they will pay you a visit. If we allow them they will take up residency and wreak havoc in our life.

During the waiting, when there is no sign of God's promises, we have to recognize that God is at work, testing our faith in this waiting period. Are we more excited about the things or Him? If we have to go months and years and no sign of His promise, are we still excited about Him and not the things?

In the "waiting" period, God doesn't want us stagnant. He wants us making preparations for what's to come, what we are expecting to see manifest in our lives. We have to live in the "now" along our journey so not to waste our lives waiting on what's to come. We can remain faithful and hold on to our hope along the way. Don't lose hope! Don't ever lose hope. Now faith is the substance of things hoped for the evidence of things not seen, that's Bible.

This waiting period reminds me of the caterpillar going through the cocoon stage of life. This is where the metamorphosis occurs, from the caterpillar stage of what we were into the butterfly stage of what we are to become. How people once saw us, slowly crawling along, just making it to the next day, on bended knees, lost, confused, slowly making our way from what was a caterpillar, into a beautiful butterfly and somewhere in between, the cocoon.

In the cocoon we need to be still. That is the time to spend in God and with Him, surrounded by His love, His grace, and His protection. This is the time when He is changing us internally, away from what people can't see, into something that will be so beautiful, for His glory.

In Chaim Bentorah's book *Hebrew Word Study* he writes about the "wait" on God's behalf and on ours:

> *The Lord will wait so that He may be gracious, and all those who wait for Him are blessed. Chakah means "to wait," "to be patient," or "to hold back." Why does God wait to bestow His favor? Why does He hold back on it? The answer that we are given is so that He can be exalted.*

Then he goes on to say:

> *"There is one additional twist to this word chakah. It is in a piel imperfect form, which implies a waiting until the last minute or even the last possible second. Sometimes, it does seem that God operates in that manner in our lives. Sarah did not have a child until it seemed too late for her to be a mother. Jericho did not fall until the seventh day. Just how is God exalted by waiting until the last minute? Think about when that last minute, or that eleventh hour, usually comes. It is when we have exhausted the last of our own resources, and the whole situation seems hopeless and impossible. At the eleventh hour, God can step in and when He does, we know that it is He – and not we – who has brought the deliverance. Then He alone is exalted.*

You know that fire that we felt when we first received the prophetic word? We have to keep it from turning into smoldering sparks. We can't lose sight of the prophetic word from God. Though it may tarry – wait on it. While in the cocoon, in the waiting period, dig deep and stir up the gift that is in you. It's not time to throw in the towel. We are changing, we are transforming. It's not time to let go of the promises of God. It's not time to leave the protection of God. We are still underdeveloped for our future, our purpose and our destiny. We have to wait on God to release us.

It's time to fight. It's time to pray for strength so that you can get through to that divine purpose and promise. It's time to grow and transform into the characteristics of Christ so that we can come out as a beautiful butterfly – free, no longer crawling but flying high above our enemies.

Bleak Circumstances

Once God shared His plans for me about being a photographer I focused on that and only that. Having that "insider" information wasn't paying the bills though. What I was to become had not manifested immediately, and therefore it was not bringing in the income to sustain the lifestyle that I created. I had a daughter graduating from high school and due to go to college, full-time, in the fall of this trying season. Though I was grateful that she would be able to attend college, I was anxious and fear began to set in as I was trying to figure out what to do to bring God's promises to pass while hanging onto His every word.

I was one of those people who dodged the phone calls from the creditors. Collecting unemployment wasn't enough. Night after night I would cry out to God, not wanting to be disobedient in taking on anything that wasn't photography.

It got to the point where I had to hide my car so it wouldn't be repossessed. One day they caught me off guard. My daughter was home and all I heard after she answered the doorbell was "mom, it's for you." On my way down the stairs of this 3-story condo she said, "Just let them take it." I think she was more fed up than I was and I never thought how my faith was affecting her.

She spent her school breaks with her father in Connecticut so in the summers I didn't care if the gas (which heated our water) got disconnected and had to endure cold showers.

If you ever had to take a cold shower unwillingly you understand my suffering. Never, ever in a million years would I wish that on anyone. The thought of standing in cold water literally gives me chills. Having to figure out the process caused me to live through these experiences.

Since my daughter wasn't there, I didn't worry as much. There were days and weeks when the electricity would get disconnected and of course there was no cable of any kind. It drew me closer to God. I am ever so grateful for my church, The Worship Center, as they helped me with a month's payment for these utilities. I made it my life's goal to give back to my church and to give in ways that will help someone else in that situation.

Summer was over and it was time to take my daughter to college. We had to go up a night before to move her in with the other freshmen the next morning. I knew I didn't have money to stay in a hotel but I never shared that with her. We loaded a car I had been "borrowing" from a friend and headed off to Syracuse, N.Y. In all of this God may not have wanted me to attend college but He allowed my daughter to attend Syracuse University. He had plans for her as well. What a proud mom I was. But never one time did I discuss God's plans for me with her. She didn't know God was taking me through this process. It never dawned on me how this could be affecting her. In her eyes she must have thought I was being irresponsible. I was on fire for God, that's all I knew. I was determined to see it through no matter what, never once counting the costs.

It was time to head to N.Y. with the borrowed car loaded with her things she needed for her freshman year. She, Diamond, and I jumped in and set out for the next chapter in our lives. The drive was six hours away. I could see the excitement in her eyes as she danced away to the music blaring in her ears from her iPod. All the while I was thinking of how I was going to manage an excuse for us having to sleep in a car and not a hotel.

That entire drive I had a six hour talking and pleading segment with God but it never made a difference. Money didn't miraculously drop from the sky or get deposited into my bank account. I had no extra money to speak of. I had only one night's reservation I could afford.

Those six hours were the longest six hours I've ever spent anywhere. I fought off the feeling of letting my daughter down. If I thought about it too much I'd end up crying and I didn't want her worrying that I was having a hard time dropping her off to college.

The feeling of disappointing her was so grueling. Knowing how hard she worked to get into Syracuse, the least I could do is have enough money to afford two nights in a hotel, what kind of mother does this to their child I kept asking myself? That was the first time it dawned on me that I never took her feelings into consideration during this career changing faith walk that I took a massive leap into. It wasn't just my life I was turning upside down; it was hers and Diamond's as well.

We made it to a hotel and in my pride I told my daughter to stay with our things, so I could go in to see if they had a room for us for that night. I knew I didn't make any reservations because I didn't have the money for it. I was in the lobby and let a few minutes pass without ever going up to the desk. Reality stung so badly and I wanted to cry out but I had to hold it together for her.

I walked back out in shame and guilt because I was now exposing my daughter to the situation MY faith got US into. I got back to the car and told her we would have to sleep in the car that night and I'd take her to her dorm the next day. I told her they didn't have any rooms available because of the state fair taking place that weekend and all the other students arriving with their families.

> *I told her we would have to sleep in the car that night.*

I decided to stay in that parking lot in hopes of remaining in a safe, lit area. I had the worst night sleep EVER. I was worried about someone breaking into the car. I felt horrible as a mom putting my daughter through such drama. That was one of the longest nights of my life. "*Weeping may endure for a night ...*" (Psalm 30:5). Before long it was morning. We awoke unharmed by any random break-ins and all of our belongings were still with us. God had kept His angels with us that entire time. Today I am still grateful.

We went to the nearest McDonald's to use their restroom to "freshen" up and to get some breakfast. God knows my heart broke in so many pieces having to go through it but also having my daughter go through it because I was trusting God for His word. I stayed the entire day getting her settled into her dorm. Her dad made it up that day to help move her in, which gave me time alone with God in the borrowed car.

I had some words with God, such as questioning if I heard Him correctly. I was questioning my faith. Now was not the time to start questioning God as He had no response for me. I did what any shameful child of God would do and apologized. I refreshed my face and went back to the dorm.

She was settled in and I got back on the road; I must have cried that entire drive. Tears of disappointment, feeling like I let my daughter down and now I was going back to a life that I had no clue as to what was going to happen next. I had to deal with readjusting to a life with a child in college. These changes were overwhelming and it was hard letting go not just of my daughter, but of life how I knew it.

Somehow I was praying through the tears while driving back to Ohio. God has such a sense of humor—over the years when I start whining and crying through my prayers, out of nowhere He would cause me to yawn. At first I thought I was tired. Then it happened with another couple of prayers. Before I could even apologize to God for yawning He said, "Your prayers are making Me tired."

"WHAT?!?" I thought, almost driving off the road hearing that response. I never offered up another crying, whining prayer to Him.

Prior to my daughter going off to college I had to pack up our house because I could no longer afford the rent. I knew she would be okay because she was in school and that gave me a few months to find a place of our own, in addition to figuring out my current financial lack. Everything we ever owned was packed up and put into a storage unit. (Want to see pictures? Visit www.rikkilwebber.com to view the gallery!)

Not Getting Any Better

After returning to Ohio I loaded up the car with the five black garbage bags that had my clothes in them. I had my important documents with me along with a few other important books and Bibles that I needed on a daily basis. Having packed up all of Diamond's belongings into the car, I turned in the keys and sat in the car contemplating what to do next. No family here in Ohio, having no place to go, no place to move in to. All I had was God's plan for my photography.

Then I headed over to a family that helped my daughter and I out when we first moved to Ohio from Maryland. We sat around the kitchen table eating dinner and I talked to them about my adventure to Syracuse and having moved all my things into storage and having the rest in the car with me. My plan was for Diamond and I to sleep in the car but they felt that was unsafe so they had me stay with them for the night. One night turned into two, and then that turned into weeks and then into months.

My daughter was done with her first semester of school and I was still without a place of our own. It was her first official break her freshman year in college and we didn't have a home of our own for her to come home to. Feelings of letting her down again came over me. Fighting back the desire to throw in the towel, I stood still in my trust in God.

This was when the struggle to be faithful became so real. When would the disappointments end? When would the pain of feeling like I wasn't a good mom going to stop? All I knew was I had to have her with me. I kept praying for God to keep us as I continued to walk out His plans for me. This part of my faith walk was new to me. I have never been in this place. This was another level of faith for me.

I knew for certain the plans that God had for me, but I didn't know the details. We walk by faith and not by sight is truly an understatement. It is very easy to say but having to live it is the challenge, at least it was for me.

I found myself between a rock and a hard place. Trying to "convince" others of what God had in store for me while nothing was manifesting. At the time people weren't seeing what I as hearing and I was having a very difficult time convincing them otherwise. It wasn't their walk of faith it was mine. I had to answer to God.

Having someone else believe in your faith doesn't put food on the table or pay the rent. I was so new at this type of faith that all I really had was my past experiences with God. He has never one time failed me. Why would He now? I kept the faith that God was going to do just what He said. The disappointment was I just thought it was going to be sooner rather than later.

I made the best of staying in people's basements and spare rooms by going to the public libraries and starting to form a business plan. This was time well spent while waiting in the cocoon. I had to find a way to do a business plan for a photography business and a financial plan to know what to do with the money on my own. Again, no college education and no money to pay a professional I had to learn to do this on my own.

Everyday I would wait for the Holy Spirit to guide me. And everyday He would provide another piece of the puzzle. I'd attend seminars and would network with other entrepreneurs all at no cost. I felt it was time well spent, building my business.

Along this journey while building my business, one of the expectations of the people that provided shelter, food and warm showers, was that I would look for work to help sustain my own place. Finding something outside of photography felt like I was being disobedient to God as that was not what He spoke to me. However, a spoken word was not providing income at this time.

Because this walk was new to me I never thought one time to look for work in photography because I never considered myself a photographer. I was blinded by doubt and fear.

It is one of the hardest things to be faithful and obedient to what God spoke, when you don't have a place of your own or enough income to supply the wait. It was either I had to find another job or we can't help you any longer. I don't blame others for not seeing what I was hearing. My faith wasn't giving them money to assist with the cost of providing food and shelter for us. These were the days and nights that I would plead with God to show up. Never having been at this place in my faith walk before I didn't know what to do. I felt disobedient to God, yet at the same time I was trying to keep myself out of a homeless shelter.

My focus was on His promise, I was stuck on that and not keeping an opened mind about ways of getting there. This is why I am sharing my story in hopes of helping at least one somebody on how to get to the promise without throwing shade your own way.

Between building these plans and job searching, it kept me quite busy. Guilt was setting in because I felt that I was being disobedient to God if I found work outside of photography. I was at a crossroad and had no clue and no right answers.

When something doesn't feel right it's a "no" to me. Yet I was missing the "yes" because I was focused on the bigger picture not the how to. The "manna" was going to waste.

Still with the never-ending question, "How's the job search going?" It was adding pressure to the guilt and betrayal. Not wanting to end up in a homeless shelter, my job search continued. I am grateful, truly grateful for the help we received during our time of need and it is my prayer that God will bless the people that helped us during those dark days.

One day while walking the neighborhood, the Holy Spirit was teaching me about wealth transfer. Each time I'd get any inspiration I'd share it with the folks helping me, but again, inspiration wasn't putting a roof over my head or paying any bills. My excitement wasn't theirs. No matter what God tells you, especially when you're going through, He will give you nuggets along the way to keep you inspired. Sometimes that's all you have to keep your dreams alive.

While building my photography business plan and searching for work, I got the devastating news. The storage company called me to tell me they were AUCTIONING off ALL OF MY BELONGINGS because I fell behind on the payments. I was done. I couldn't ask for any more help than what I was getting. How do I go to anyone else for $895 to keep my things from being auctioned off? I was so broken I couldn't breathe. My life was in that storage unit.

"God, you never said it would be like this. Where are You? Where are the things that You promised me? I am struggling to find work. I am not living in my own place. This is not what You said Your plans were for my life. God, why have You forsaken me?" Ever been there? Ever felt that God was so far away that you felt helpless and in despair? And all you were doing was being obedient to what He told you, to what He shared with you? Hopeless, homeless, and lost all of our possessions were not in the blueprint.

> *God, where are you? Where are the things you promised me?*

If I even start to list the things or try to remember everything that was in that storage unit it would drudge up all the bad memories so please take my word for it, my life and my daughter's life was in that unit. I reached out to them in hopes of working out any arrangements but they were not open to them. And then the Holy Spirit said to me, "Without fail you will recover it all." I wasn't feeling it but that was the word that kept me from going to the grave. It took me a few days of encouraging myself to get back to my new reality.

After receiving that news about the storage I was then told that my favor from the family that was helping us had run out. It was time for me to find another place to live. They gave me a month to find work or it was time for us to go. They did what they could for us and I am forever grateful.

A month came and went and no work. I was able to find another place to stay with another family. "God, why was this my life? Were there lessons I was missing along the way that may have prolonged the process?

Was I brought out to Ohio to live with families and not on my own?" This was not my mission in life.

Hope and a Promise

Finally, after a couple of months with the next family I was able to find work. Not work in photography, but it was work that provided income.

This job was part-time, and in walking distance. The walking worked in my favor as it kept me in shape. Having no transportation at this point, not even a borrowed car, walking 3.5 miles each way kept me fit. It allowed me time with God. He was sharing so many things with me. It gave me hope and encouragement. He shared more details of my future but not the steps to get there. Strangely it brought me closer to God even in these trying times because the not knowing how caused me to act in faith. Daily I had to rely on God to turn these dark days into glorious days.

I walked to and from work each day rain or shine, heat or cold. I found shorter ways to get to work and it allowed me to see the new houses going up around the area in which one day He said I will have a house in New Albany of my own.

Sleeping in cars, staying in houses that weren't ours, losing my possessions and having no transportation were very humbling experiences for me. Never thought that the story would unfold the way that it has. Where my faith has led me to my current situation was great cause to give up. However; no one will ever accuse me of being a quitter.

Accepting NO Limits

Chapter Two
The Early Years

Dream: *Chalam*

"In a dream, in a vision of the night, when deep sleep falls upon men, while slumbering on their beds, then He opens the ears of men, and seals their instruction."
~ JOB 33:15-16 NKJV

"And it shall come to pass afterward that I will pour out My Spirit on all flesh; your sons and your daughters shall prophesy, your old men shall dream dreams, your young men shall see visions."
~ JOEL 2:28 NKJV

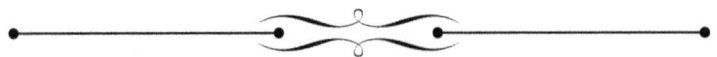

I am a firm believer that God uses dreams to communicate to us, especially while we are asleep. Then and only then is God in complete control over our mind and thoughts.

As far back as I can remember, even before I knew there was a God or who God was, I was a dreamer. I want to take you on a journey back to my earlier years, as far back as I can remember, and show you how I was introduced to God and how my relationship with Him began.

Some of you may not agree with my beliefs or religion and that's okay, but this is about what I went through. I am not trying to persuade you to change your beliefs or the god you serve.

My testimony is based on the God that I serve. I am fully persuaded that God alone has kept me. God has delivered me from other people's opinions years ago. Now, let us journey on.

My story isn't one of being born and raised in the church. As I recall, every now and again, we would visit a church here and there when I was very young. Then in my teenage years, our Sundays would consist of my sisters and I going to the local laundromat to do the weekly laundry for the entire family (eight people to be exact).

Every Sunday we were awakened at 6:00 a.m. so we could get to the laundromat as soon as they opened and so we weren't in there all day waiting on machines. (At least that was my mother's theory. Mine would have been to sleep in and then take my chances with the availability of the community machines.)

One of my earliest memories of any church, was being in a Sunday school class, perhaps around the age of 8 or 9. In this class we sat around and discussed Noah's Ark. Not going to church on a regular basis, I had nothing to connect Noah's story to or any other story in the Bible. To me it was as if I was in a History class at school. At the time, it didn't make much sense to me why a man had to take his family and a bunch of animals in a boat away from all the people to go and start a new nation of people. Why couldn't they just stay where they were and live with the people there? Not being a regular attender and not hearing the entire story in context, this caused great confusion on my behalf about God and His instructions to His people.

While at this church I don't recall ever officially becoming a member the way that I know it today. We must have attended awhile at this church, because I recall my sisters being in the Christmas play one year. After that Christmas play I don't remember anything else about that church.

At this time I knew nothing about having faith in God. The results of not having a personal relationship with God or studying His word can bring about misunderstanding of who He really is and the history is of Christianity. It gets complicated to make connections on any level when you are disconnected.

Growing up in a home that didn't attend nor have I belonged to a church I had no firm spiritual foundation. I had no point of reference on how God uses dreams and visions to communicate to us as found in Genesis 37:5 NKJV. As a child, I would dream a lot. I don't mean just a few nights a year. It was and still is to the point that when I don't dream it's not normal. Because of this, I have been dubbed "Josephina" the female version of Joseph in the Bible. It became clear to me that this was God's way of communicating to me. I don't question His reasons for choosing this way of communicating with me. I have learned to go with God's flow. Later in life I have discovered that this was considered having the gift of a "Seer."

In Chaim Bentorah's book *Hebrew Word Study* he says this about seeing what God sees regarding dreams:

> *The sages taught that during sleep, your soul is active and not influenced by the physical body. It is during this time that God can become intimate with your soul. In such intimacy, you will see what God sees. God sees the past, the present, and the future. Thus, a byproduct of this intimate time with God is that we get to see what He sees, including the future.*
>
> *The sages go on to teach that if we were really to see exactly as God sees, we would not be able to endure it, especially in terms of the future. Therefore, He wraps our dreams in symbols so that we will not be too startled by what we see. In many cases, He will not allow us to remember a dream because the knowledge of our intimacy with Him would be too shocking for us to endure. God will "seal" our instruction. He will give us a dream, have an intimate moment with us, and then bury what He has shared in symbolism or cause us to forget it completely.*

At this time in my life I didn't know that God had a voice. I don't remember being taught that He had a Son, Jesus. We celebrated Christmas but not as the birth of Christ. As a child these dreams came to me but I didn't know to say anything about them. Not knowing to journal these dreams and visions, I would just wake up and think about them at times and eventually most of them would be a distant memory, if that, as I had no use for them, so I thought.

My Super Power

I can recall times as a kid, that our family would take road trips to sporting events or to see family outside of Connecticut. I recall on a few of those trips, I would be in a window seat in our station wagon, looking out the window, thinking how some of these places looked strangely familiar.

From time to time I would yell out, "hey, I've been here before." One of these road trips we were on our way to New York City to see the New York Yankees, which was my father's favorite baseball team. I remember looking out the window as we were driving along and thinking how the buildings looked when I was there before, on my own, no family trip that time. Whenever this happened it always felt like déjà vu. I was not understanding it was a dream coming to pass. Though I didn't know God or have any known relationship with Him, this didn't prevent Him from preparing me for my purpose.

Being in the city, it all looked the same from the time that I was there before, through a dream, the view through a car window, admiring the city of Manhattan. This was so real to me that I remembered this was not my first trip to New York City. I was too young to understand how dreams would become reality. Somehow my future collided with my past and created my present, that's what dreams are made of.

I believed that if I made it hundreds of miles away from home, alone, that I must have had super or special powers to transport myself from Connecticut to NYC without anyone ever knowing. Not giving up on my attempt to persuade my family that I wasn't crazy, that I had been to NYC before, I can remember my brothers teasing me about being stupid and watching too much television.

> *I must have had special powers to transport me from Connecticut to New York City.*

Nowhere in my thought process did I connect these events in my dreams to God. I had no spiritual guidance to bring me to that conclusion. I believed my mother when her interpretation was "maybe you are reincarnated." Not understanding at the time what reincarnated really meant, that became the topic of conversation the remainder of the trip, until we pulled up into the parking lot of Yankee Stadium. After hearing that I was reincarnated, I could no longer think about the baseball game. My entire focus was now on what I was before I became Rikki from Connecticut? This theory has stuck with me my entire life. Now I just get a chuckle out of it. As a child though we believe what our parents say to us until we reach the stage of discovery.

I Was A Dolphin

I was physically sitting in the baseball stadium. As the game was being played I could hear the sounds of the crowd cheering and booing and hear the amazing sound of the bat meeting the ball and seeing the players running around the bags. But this particular hot summer afternoon mentally I was absent. I had more important matters to think about.

My mind began to wander, coming up with strange ideas about being reincarnated. Perhaps I was a dolphin or a lion or maybe even a tree. What appealed to me the most, was the idea of having been a dolphin. This is why after all of those years I consider dolphins to be my favorite animal. I wanted to believe that I was something that was peaceful, graceful, and had no worries in life, at least in my mind. So, it was settled, I was a dolphin in my previous life.

I wanted to believe that I was something that was peaceful, graceful, and had no worries in life.

What's so hilarious to me about this rationale is that I don't even swim like a dolphin. Having had swimming lessons as a child, I had a near drowning experience during one of those lessons. At least it seemed that way to me. In this particular swimming lesson that day we were using the kickboards. I relied on those boards to keep me from going under water.

We were told to stretch out and start kicking as fast as we could while holding onto the board. I didn't realize that as my feet were kicking there were enormous splashes flying over my body, crashing down on my head. In a panic I was screaming, "Help me, I'm drowning," all the while I was holding onto the kickboard.

I was more nervous than drowning but to me it felt like I couldn't breathe and never wanted to swim again. Oh, I still go in the water even as an adult but I am one of those head over the top of the water kind of swimmers. How's that for ever being a dolphin in my previous life?

The Dark Side

Still no church home, I was left with the daunting task of resolving the mystery of seeing dreams. Years passed and we started attending a Unitarian Meeting House, known for its "stimulating worship services." Not knowing my exact age at this time I am going to take a wild guess and say maybe 13.

To my recollection, my maternal grandparents were members of a Unitarian Meeting House which is why this was familiar ground to my mom and her family. We were going where she was comfortable to worship at the time.

We began attending this church every Sunday. It kept us from having to do laundry at the crack of dark every Sunday morning. So for now I was okay with it. We attended the morning services, as sometimes they would have afternoon and/or evening services. I cannot say that all Unitarian Meeting Houses are the same as we only attended this one.

From what I remember the services would start with us singing from the hymnals, and to this very day *In the Garden* is my favorite hymn.

Then there was a greeting / welcome from one of the three ministers leading the service. I don't remember reading from a Bible during the service. Then it came time for the "message." Now, the services that I attended never had anyone reading from the Bible or preaching from one. I don't remember hearing a scripture being read to us. This is all from what I can recall. If they did I really don't remember as this was over 37 years ago. If I'm recalling incorrectly then charge it to my head and not my heart.

The message would consist of three ministers standing and pacing in front of the front row until they heard a voice or saw a face in the spirit. The very first service I became intrigued, as this was my first experience with people being interactive with voices they were hearing. Then suddenly one of the three would start sharing with the congregation what they were hearing or seeing in the spirit realm. Good or evil, the spirit realm is real, read 1 Samuel 28.

At times they would describe someone they were "seeing" or start asking people if they knew of a "Mary" or a "Harold." This went on for quite some time throughout the service. When they no longer heard or saw anything then the message was over. We would sing, take up an offering and leave.

Many people stayed around talking to others after the service. The ones who received a message sometimes stayed to ask for clarity or to see if these ministers could continue to talk to their families or friends that they saw earlier in the spirit. I always stayed in the back row and would be ready to head out into the halls away from these encounters.

I didn't understand then why I wasn't embracing these encounters during these services. It is evident that God had His hands on me my entire life. He has kept me from going into the dark side. I was always uneasy, never had peace in any of these services. God was preparing me and covering me during this time because He had a purpose for me. People can conjure up spirits of the dead but that's not what God wanted for my life. This is why He was making me uneasy during those services.

"Gut feeling" comes to mind when I start to sense a spirit of being uneasy. When there is no peace in the things that I choose to do then I don't continue in them. I was becoming sensitive to the Holy Spirit and how I was going to encounter Him in my future without knowing where this road was leading me.

> *When there is no peace in the things that I choose to do then I don't continue in them.*

Messages From the Dead

After having that first encounter with the "dead" I was afraid of going back to that church. When fear is involved, that's a sure sign to me that God isn't. My mom insisted we attend and being under the age of 18 and living under her roof I had no choice. I would always sit in the very back row as I didn't want anyone telling me that someone "dead" was speaking to them to tell me something that I needed to know or was going to happen to me.

Little did I realize that no matter where I sat, I couldn't hide from spirits. Good or evil, they are all around. Daily I now ask for God's protection from all kinds of evil. No harm shall come against my dwelling place or me. That includes my daughter as well.

One service I was in the very back row and still got called out. This "message" was from a family member that had gone on to another life. This woman stood at the front of the church, pointed me out, "you, young lady in the red." As she pointed at me I turned around to see who else had on red. No one even close to me was wearing red. I slide down in my seat as far as I could, being that I was 5'7".

"You, you in the red," she said again. "I am hearing that you are a teacher." I have no recollection if she had anything else to say to me as I was stuck on me being a teacher. I never had the thought of ever wanting to be a teacher. At that age, I only thought of being a veterinarian at first and then that changed to being an architect. Nowhere in there did I ever want to be a teacher. "Hah" I thought, "I got her." She said a teacher not a veterinarian.

When they had "messages" for other people, I didn't know if it were true or not as I didn't know any of them personally. I knew for sure they had it all wrong about me so from that point on I knew whatever "dead" people they were talking to that it all had to be made up.

The afternoon/evening services would consist of "readings" of our palms or more "messages" but in a one on one setting, because these services were held in the overflow area of the church. I enjoyed going to these services because there was always food. We had to purchase tickets for these "extra" services.

> *God doesn't want us bound by divinations, like horoscopes.*

One day I purchased a ticket and had my palm read. She told me about meeting a tall dark man. "Hah," again. Did she not know that in the projects where we were living in Hartford, Connecticut that's ALL that lived in that neighborhood? Everyday I would wait for one of those tall dark men. It NEVER happened.

If we are not careful, divination can control our thought process and our lives if we allow it to. God doesn't want us bound by divinations, like horoscopes. He wants us to have encounters with Him. To be free to do His will. Free of fear and anxiety.

Those younger years came and went with me still having dreams, even while in high school. From time to time in the halls, I would hear about church. I didn't want to hear about a church because of the encounters I had at the Unitarian Meeting House. It just left an uneasy feeling with me. I didn't want to see a church; I didn't want to know that church existed. To me all of them were the same. I had my fill of hearing from the spirit realm.

More Spirits

I stayed clear of anyone that I heard was attending church at all. We were back to the days of being "bedside Baptist" and "mattress Methodist." We didn't have a church to attend at that time. I'm not completely sure why we stopped attending. I was ecstatic that we weren't going anymore. I'd take the days of doing laundry at 6:00 a.m. over sitting in a service, much afraid.

At some point my dad started attending Hopewell Baptist Church. He never went to the Unitarian Meeting House with us. One day I remember him asking us to go to church with him. He said that this church was different from any other churches we ever attended. I don't know why to this day that we weren't told to go but he "asked" us to go. I understand now that it was a delay in me meeting the one true God.

One Sunday I gave in and attended with him. I sat in the congregation as he was seated in the choir stand. He loved to sing, and had an amazing voice, that's why he was in the choir. When the choir got up to sing the energy grew in the church. Not ever being in a Baptist church before, I didn't understand the "move" of the Spirit at that time. All I remember was I was watching my dad sing with a great big smile on his face and then suddenly he "fainted." With these experiences and encounters in church services, it's a wonder I would ever go again.

Later, in the car ride back home he explained to me that this was the "move" of the "Holy Spirit." Oh great, here we go again, more spirits.

I went that one time and never again. I didn't want anything to do with any spirits in church services. So one Sunday morning when my dad left for church I stayed in my mom's rocking chair in the living room and rocked while waiting for him to come back home from church. He loved to sing and had an amazing voice, that's why he was in the choir.

I stayed in my mom's chair, rocking for so long while waiting on him to get home that I started to wear the carpet out. Hours went by and he finally made it home. Who would want to be in church on a Sunday for four or five hours?

He would walk in the door singing what the choir sang or a song that stuck in his spirit. He didn't look anxious or fearful. He looked peaceful and happy. Though he was happy, I had those early encounters etched in my memory so I was content with the rocking chair and my Michael Jackson LP's on Sunday mornings.

Senior year had come and gone and I was certain that I was done with church and I was off to the business school in New Haven, CT. Unaware that I was walking out God's plans for me all along.

The school provided apartment housing in place of dorms on a campus since the school was in a former office building, which did not allow for dormitory spacing. This was fine with me as it created a sense of independence away from home. This became my home for the next nine months. God was nurturing something spiritually inside of me during this nine-month period.

The Early Years

Roommates

At the age of 18 I had set a goal for myself to see all 50 States of America. I had big dreams for myself and traveling was one of them. Moving to New Haven was the beginning of my life of traveling. Here I was being drawn to the very thing that God had placed in me as part of my destiny, that directional pull without understanding why.

Before I could live the life as a traveler I had to graduate from this business school. A couple of months passed, school had been good to me so far. Much to my surprise, four women in a two-bedroom apartment hadn't been so bad. We all got along really well and today I am still in touch with one of those roommates.

With the bond we were creating through this living arrangement we all decided not to go home on the weekends. We explored the city and our surroundings. I was not realizing that God was developing something spiritual inside of me during these nine months I was spending time with other believers and getting to know them and not their religion.

It was a couple of weeks before I knew two of them were Christians. Not that they were ashamed. They lived by example. There were nights we would sit in the living room talking late into the night, sharing stories of our childhood and families. One night they found out I didn't attend a church but never asked me about being a believer of Jesus Christ.

What I love and respect about them to this day is they never forced their God on us. The two roommates that attended church were always around the apartment singing. Their songs never sound familiar to me and I later discovered that it was because they were Gospel songs.

What I love and respect about them to this day is they never forced their God on us.

One night God set me up. These ladies told me they were going to a concert. I was all up for concerts. When I heard "concert" and living in New Haven you didn't ask or care who was performing because everyone was good. They knew I was into music because my bedroom walls, at least the two on my side of the room, had wall-to-wall posters and cutout pictures of the one and only, Michael Jackson. I had so many pictures up of him that you couldn't see any parts of the walls.

I told them I wanted to go so we got dressed and were off to have a night of fun, music, and dancing, at least that's how I saw the night going. Unknowingly, this was going to be the night that would change the rest of my life!

We pulled up to the building and I was perplexed because it was a church, not an arena, concert hall or civic center. Certainly this was a mistake. Maybe they wanted to offer up a prayer before we went to the actual concert? However, they parked the car instead of pulling up to the curb to jump out for a Hail Mary. They intended to stay here, for the concert.

I had two choices. I could go in with them and find out what kind of concert I was in for, or I could walk back to our apartment. Not having any idea where in New Haven we were, I had no money for a cab and at that time there was no GPS or Uber. Sitting in the car was not an option as it was cold, and in the New England area cold is not your friend. I was left to the one obvious choice, so I headed inside the church with trepidation.

The Concert

All of the memories of my past church experiences were coming back to me like a flood. My palms were sweating and my heart was beating at a rapid pace. What was I getting myself into? Why were my feet leading

The Early Years

me back into a church? I swore off church years ago! Help! Someone make my feet stop moving.

But then both roommates walked on either side of me, grabbed ahold of my arms, and told me that it would be a night I would never forget. They said that the music would be life changing and that they would be with me the entire night. I was still unaware that this was a Gospel concert because I had never been to one. All I knew is I did not want to ever step foot in a church again. Yet here I was heading straight for the front door.

I just needed to get past the fear and get through the doors to know that it could be life changing. "Help me, I'm drowning," is what this felt like all over again. With much hesitation, I took a deep breath and felt that I could trust them. With two very strong spirited young ladies by my side I took my first step into my Divine destiny.

Finally having made our way inside, it resembled a fashion show. Big hats, amazing dresses and suits- it was straight out of a magazine. I had never been to anything like this in my entire life. It was so glamorous. I believe if Danielle Steel was a Christian writer she'd write about the lives like these. I felt like I had stepped onto a movie scene. The women were so elegant and the men were dressed like Emmy nominees. I later discovered that this fashion sense came from people wearing their best for God.

The lights went dim and the music began to play. Then, just like a secular concert a group of people came out to sing. I was told that this was the "choir" and that a guy named Richard Smallwood was the "director." Not knowing him or ever hearing any of these terms regarding music and church it was my initiation into live Gospel music.

I noticed that the atmosphere began to change. I had never seen anything like it.

As the concert went on I noticed that the atmosphere began to change. I had never seen anything like it. It was starting to get extremely warm in the church. Fans were being passed around and people started sweating out from under those big hats, beautiful dresses and suits. And then some people began yelling and screaming. Not the kind of yelling and screaming where you feel threatened. It was one of excitement, of worship and praise. The heat must have gotten to most of them because then people began to "dance," "shout," and run around the building. Immediately I thought, "oh boy, they are seeing dead people." Clearly I hadn't been delivered from my past, and yet this was only the beginning.

Though my thoughts transported me back to my previous experiences with the church, I didn't feel uncomfortable. I wasn't afraid this time. There was a sense of calm that came over me. From time to time when my roommates weren't up dancing and clapping they would check in with me to see if I was okay. Neither they nor I had any idea that God had birthed something inside of me long before that night; He was doing a work on the inside of me. I sat and watched, I was what they call a "spectator" in the church. I don't recall all of the songs that were sung, but there was one song in particular that stuck with me that night. It had such a catchy jingle to it and the beat just took over my soul.

It was when a group of women took to the "stage" by the name of the Clark Sisters. They sang a song entitled *I'm Looking for a Miracle*. I remember rocking and bobbing my head to the beat as if I was familiar with this song. That song got so deep into my spirit without my knowledge and was filed into my memory bank. Like the days when my dad came home from church singing a song that stuck with his spirit. It is said if you want to remember something put it to a song. "A, b, c, d, e, f, g..." I bet I got you singing the alphabet instead of saying it didn't I (LOL).

"I'm looking for a miracle, I expect the impossible, I feel the intangible & I see the invisible. The sky is the limit to what I can have. Just believe and

receive it, God will perform it today." Unknowingly, that song became the foundation for my Divine destiny. I still declare it, I live it and I receive it, today.

The attendees praised their way through the night, with a burning in their soul. Jeremiah said "it's like fire shot up in my bones."

My roommates talked about the entire concert on the way back to our apartment and entertained all of my questions. They explained to me about the move of the Holy Spirit. They talked about what a privilege it was to have both Richard Smallwood and the Clark Sisters at the same concert. I didn't know any of them but I would never forget them or that night.

We were so wound up when we got back to the apartment that none of us wanted to retire for the evening. We sat up and talked about everything under the sun. They asked me about church but I told them I wasn't ready to discuss my experiences, in fact, I wanted to forget about the church experiences I had. I didn't know everything about what God had in store for me after that night but I know my life had never been the same. One thing for certain; He has had His hand on me the entire time.

Looking For A Miracle

The next holiday weekend was upon us and I went home, as did my roommates. That weekend I remember it vividly, like it was just yesterday. Back home I was walking around the house singing, "I'm looking for a miracle." I sang it so much my mom got tired of hearing me and yelled at me a number of times to stop singing it. Something inside of me just wouldn't let it go. When my dad heard it, he told me that they sing songs like that in his church and I should go back. I was still traumatized by the speaking and hearing from the dead that I didn't want to find out that his church did the same. I was not ready at that time to give it a try. I was being processed.

While still home on break, we went bowling one night and as we were bowling, I found myself singing that song over and over and over again. My cousins and sisters inquired of the song and I told them I heard it at a concert while down at school. My mom said, "She won't stop singing that song. It's driving me crazy!" God was using me to plant seeds into their lives as well. The harvest that was yet to yield from this planting.

God was using me to plant seeds into their lives as well. The harvest that was yet to yield from this planting.

Still seeing dreams in the night, still going places in my dreams where I've never been and people I've never seen and still not understanding why I was a dreamer. It was something I couldn't change nor wanted to. I would see events that hadn't happened. I would see into the future and it gave me hope. There were questions still unanswered. There were pieces still missing. The only difference was I no longer felt like I was reincarnated but now I was on a mission to find out why I was a dreamer.

My roommates always attended church on the Sundays they stayed at the apartment and never missed a service. They never imposed themselves or bugged me to go. They knew that one day, if it were meant to be, when I was ready, I would go. I never did attend any other Gospel concerts or church services with them. The process was being worked out in me.

I Have Never Been The Same

Fast-forward a year after completing business school and I find myself working two jobs, a full-time and part-time job to manage a life on my own. While working the part-time job there was someone who talked to me every day (three times a week) about having a relationship with God. They never, ever gave up. When we have a relationship with God, we want to share Him with others so they can have what we have, and that's eternal life.

Finally I caved. I went to the church so this person would leave me alone. It's funny how God will use people to get on your nerves in order to move you in the direction we should go in the first place.

This church experience was like no other. This wasn't a Gospel concert this time. This was a Sunday morning worship service. In a lot of ways it was quite the same setting and atmosphere as the concert. People were always standing, praising, singing, crying, running and even "shouting." The worship service didn't have as many selections as the concert but the atmosphere was the same. I started to see the connection of the two settings.

At this worship service, what struck me was the "message" from the preacher that morning. He said things that I never heard spoken from a pulpit until that day. He talked about a Man named Jesus Christ. He talked about how He was God's Son and about "sins" and living right. Never in my life had I heard anything like it in the churches where I attended at a younger age. At this time in my life I was 19 years old, and that's when my past collided with my future and became my present. All of the preparation and going through the process of overcoming my past led me to this day.

That worship service stuck with me. It was changing something on the inside of me that I couldn't explain. I didn't understand it all. I just knew I was drawn in. I went a couple more Sundays and one Sunday I was sitting three rows from the front. Not feeling the need to hide, I was no longer afraid of going to church. Then, as I was listening to the sermon, tears began to stream down my face. My heart rate became very rapid and my palms began to sweat. It was the same feeling I felt outside the concert that night in New Haven. The Holy Spirit got a hold of me.

I found myself walking up the aisle to publicly accept Jesus Christ as my personal Savior. Since that day, that moment, I have never been the same. My life began to align with God's will for my life. I then realized I had so much to be delivered from my earlier experiences and my times at the Unitarian Meeting House. It was now time for me to learn about this God I just accepted into my life. For the very first time I was now an official member of a church. Now I was a born again, baptized believer, at First Baptist Church in Hartford, Connecticut.

The quest of finding out more about God and His Son and the Holy Spirit had begun. I'm not sure why but for some reason I missed a couple of weeks after shortly becoming a member of FBC. When I returned I remember that I was sitting in the center of the church almost close to the very back. This was one habit I had to break, "hiding" like I did in the other church. I didn't know anyone there to sit with, didn't have any family attending at the time nor had I made any friends, yet, so I sat where there was room and where I was comfortable.

It was time for the "greeting" and the pastor was looking around acknowledging the guests that attended that day. Then it happened. I heard him say, "Baby, where have you been?" Now, there are about 500 people in this place but he was looking in a particular direction, MINE.

I had no idea how he even saw that far back in the church. People began to turn around so I followed suit- I turned around as well. Apparently the person he was addressing was not sitting behind me. Since his question wasn't answered he decided he'd add a description to the person in which he was addressing. "No, you in the blue with the big gold hoop earrings on." People began to look around, as did I and then it felt like I was transported back to my early years of wearing the red and being called out. In shear horror, I realized he was talking to me. The 6% of Irish that is in me caused me to turn "beet red." I don't have to see when I get flushed because I can feel the blood rushing to my face.

In one regard it was nice to know that I was missed. In another, I was on pins and needles thinking he too was going to tell me that the spirit of a relative of mine was coming back to give me a "word" for my future. Oh the demons and awful memories that flashed before me.

I wanted so desperately to slide down in my seat and hide but instead, a feeling of calm came over me and I suddenly began to realize that something was helping me in stressful moments like these. Boy, did I have so much to learn about God the Father, God the Son, and God the Holy Spirit.

The pastor never waited to hear my response, as I don't believe I could have come up with one even if I had it written on a cue card in front of me. He went on and told the congregation that it is important to come as often as we can so not to be vulnerable to the attacks of the enemy while being away from the church. That was the day I learned how to be a consistent attendee of my church.

The devil constantly attacks us when we are disconnected from other believers.

The devil constantly attacks us when we are disconnected from other believers. Having the strength to make it day to day comes from our Power Source. In order to run on full we have to remain connected to the Source.

> *"Not forsaking the assembling of ourselves together, as is the manner of some, but exhorting one another, and so much the more as you see the Day approaching."*
> ~ HEBREWS 10:25.

From that day forward, I only missed Sundays if I was either sick or traveling. I became adamant about never missing a Sunday service without these reasons. God has been so good to me; He has done so much for me. He saved me from spending an eternity in hell. As long as I have breath in my body, you will always find me in the house of God giving Him the praise that is due His name.

Now having become a member of a church I felt anchored. I belonged here. Something inside of me wasn't satisfied with just having a church home. I knew deep down inside, there was something more to just attending church. With my past church experiences and my dreams it was time for me to gather as much information as I could to find a deeper understanding.

For me it's just not merely enough to accept a condition or situation as is. There is a reason, a purpose in it. Sometimes it may not be for me to find it, but the process of discovery helps to shape my character in becoming more like Christ. Faith and patience help mold me each time. For all these years that I've had those dreams, it was God communicating to me, leading and guiding me even before I knew He existed. He'll equip us for our journey even before we know we are on a journey. After all, I'm looking for a miracle, I expect the impossible.

Chapter Three
Internal Reconstruction

Awaken: *Quts*

"As for me, I will see Your face in righteousness; I shall be satisfied when I awake in Your likeness."
- PSALM 17:15 NKJV

"If My people who are called by My name will humble themselves, and pray and seek My face, and turn from their wicked ways, then I will hear from heaven, and will forgive their sin and heal their land."
- 2 CHRONICLES 7:14 NKJV

After giving my life to Christ at First Baptist Church, it was now time to find out what being "saved" really meant. Having spent my entire life crawling through it like a caterpillar, it was now time for me to head into the cocoon stage. I needed to know, what was this talk about repentance and having a spiritual life? The times that I had been in church for the concert and worship services, the calm that came over me, what was this "warm" feeling that I was experiencing inside? So many things were new to me; I was now on a mission for a deeper understanding of it all.

There are a whole lot of things that people can say about me. Some may be true, some may be pure gossip birthed from a spirit of jealousy. However, one sure thing that can be said about me is that I am persistent.

Not having all the answers to my questions and being new to the congregation, I didn't know anyone in the church at the time to help guide me or become a mentor to me. So I began my research. I attended every service they offered, I was in every Sunday school class that was provided and, attended Bible Study every week. I even attended weekday prayer services that started at 6:00 a.m. Being a morning person, this didn't bother me in the least. It actually created a good habit of praying before my day got started and a habit I continue to this day. "The early bird catches the worm." I start first thing in the morning before the world awakens to get my uninterrupted time in with God.

Now I was on a mission to seek answers to all of my questions. I was attending classes, being present at the worship services, Bible studies, and prayer services- I had an awakening in my spirit. The "old" me couldn't reside with the "new" me. I came to the understanding that I had to be delivered from people engaging with the spirits of people that have passed away. I was learning that there is One Spirit, the Holy Spirit. The Holy Spirit is the only One that I want to hear and talk to, and He is the only One spirit that I wanted a spiritual relationship with. Hearing so much about Him and understanding that He being a "person" not a "thing" had made me very uncomfortable to think that I had to interact with any spirits at all. However; from my findings I discovered that He is a gentle Spirit, and will not force Himself on anyone. The Holy Spirit was sent as a Comforter, an Advocate, a Counselor, to be with us after the ascension of Jesus Christ (John 14:16).

My spiritual man began to grow and became stronger in the Bible. However, I still had so many unanswered questions. I took my search to another level; I began researching through books! A man once said about African-Americans, "If you want to hide something from them, put it in a book." It took only one time for me to know that and I made it my life's journey to always read. How ironic that I am now an Author. God's ways are not our ways, nor His thoughts our thoughts.

One of the greatest resources that we have at our disposal is a book. Everything and anything can be found in a book. You just have to be mindful of what books you are feeding your inner man (your spirit man). In 1984, (that's the year I accepted Christ as my personal Lord and Savior) we didn't have access to the Internet like we do now. Fortunately, First Baptist had a bookstore in the church. I want to reiterate, if you want to learn something new, pick up a book. If you want to broaden your horizons, pick up a book. If you think you are at a point where you have more knowledge to offer than what's available, write a book. Someone, somewhere may

If you want to broaden your horizons, pick up a book. If you think you are at a point where you have more knowledge to offer than what's available, write a book.

be waiting on the knowledge that you have to offer by writing a book to set him or her free.

In Chaim Bentorah's book *Hebrew Word Study* when David said, *"As for me, I will see Your face in righteousness; I shall be satisfied when I awake in Your likeness"* (Psalm 17:15 NKJV). Chaim writes:

> *"David is saying that while he is alive on earth, he will behold (see) God's face. The Hebrew word for "face" is pani, which is often rendered as "God's presence." The word for "behold" has two possible roots. If we say the root is chazah, which means "to see" or "to perceive," we would have to render pani as "face" – thus saying that David is actually seeing the face of God. However, if we say that the roos is 'achaz, which means "to seize" or "to grab hold of," we would then more correctly render pani as "presence," which would make more sense. Rather than David seeing the face of God, he is seizing or holding on to the presence of God."*

> *"That is why I can relate to the following rendering much more easily: "As for me, while I live on this earth, I am going to hold on to the presence of God. When I awake into heaven, I will be satisfied to see His likeness," or "to see Him face-to-face." The word for "satisfied" in Hebrew is sava, which is also the word for "seven" and for "complete filling" or "completeness." Thus, in heaven, we will be made complete, or be completely filled – not only by experiencing God's presence but also by actually seeing Him."*

"Being in God's presence, getting in God's face, feeling His presence in your life" are things that I heard in my very early years as a Christian. My question was, "how do you get in God's presence/face when you can't see Him in the natural?" This was the start of my spiritual (internal) reconstruction. My inner man, spirit man, had to be reconstructed to have the same characteristics as Christ. In the former church we attended, I saw how people paced the floor, humming and sometimes lying on the floor in order to "feel the presence of a spirit" that they had been waiting on to appear. Their eyes were always closed, appearing to be in a trance of some sort at times. These things were imparted to me at a very young age and left a very uneasy, uncomfortable feeling whenever I heard anything about "spirits." How was God going to reconstruct this mixed up inner man in me? He certainly had His work cut out for Him in my life.

The Cocoon Stage

My spirit needed a firm foundation. One that would take deep roots and never to be shaken by my past. *"That we should no longer be children, tossed to and fro and carried about with every wind of doctrine, by the trickery of men, in the cunning craftiness of deceitful plotting"* (Ephesians 4:14 NKJV). It was time to feed my spirit man so it would no longer be a child tossed from here to there. It was time to mature in the spirit.

Might I add, building a foundation of this magnitude may not be for everyone. Like any physical structure, we all have options. Builders have different designs for different owners. The deeper your pockets the deeper the foundation. As with the spiritual foundation, your purpose will match your foundation. By design, the deeper you go into your spiritual study the higher you'll go in God. How much time are you willing to SPEND in study, in prayer, in His presence, to build a stronger spiritual foundation?

I am truly grateful that out of all the places I could have started my spiritual journey, out on it was at First Baptist Church. The teaching, the preaching and the resources were all made available for new members, and for continued growth for the seasoned members. Those that took advantage of these offerings were building a stronger spiritual foundation.

I appreciated having a church to call so much, home that I made it a point to always be present. I was showing gratitude to God for loving me so much, that He sent His Son to die in my place. After all, the story of my youth could have led me down an entirely different path had I not gone down the one that I did. I am truly grateful.

Anytime the church doors were opened I was there. I made it a point to be in the bookstore, on a weekly basis. The hunger for more knowledge and my continued growth in Christ was strong in my early years. The more I read, the more I could see a change in me. The way I walked, the way I talked. The people I hung out with, the places I would go, all of that started to change. I wasn't the same person I was before accepting Christ. No, I wasn't perfect but I certainly was not the same. Praise God the "old" man passed away! All I kept hearing from family and friends was, "why are you always in church?" That was funny to me. What better place to be than to be in church ALL OF THE TIME? I could have been accused of much worse.

After all my time in the bookstore, I had books every place I turned. Books were in my car, on every floor in my apartment, at my job and in the bathroom. I had books on prayer, on the presence of God, on spiritual discernment, on demons and on breaking generational curses. You name it, I had it. As I continued feeding my spirit, I continued to grow stronger, more confident, spiritually. I began to notice a change in me, emotionally. My transformation into a butterfly had begun. I wasn't the shy, quiet person I used to be. I finally had something and someone to be passionate about. Wanting more of God was taking over my life, in a good, strong way. The more I wanted, the more He gave. Not realizing that He was preparing me for my destiny.

> *The more I wanted the more He gave.*

It was there on Greenfield Street, in Hartford, Connecticut, that I learned what being in God's presence truly meant. Prayer was that access that got me in the presence of the almighty God. It wasn't easy. Prayer is a two way street. When we pray, we are communicating with God. Since

God is not in human form, that meant He was in the spiritual realm. Having to talk to a spirit, even the Holy Spirit, wasn't easy for me. But the more I wanted, the more He gave. Gently, patiently, in His ever-loving way, God helped me, one day at a time, to get past my past.

At first a state of paranoia took over, as did doubt and fear. Doubt that I was even hearing the Holy Spirit and fear that now I was dabbing into "witchcraft" by communicating with spirits at all. The more I read about spiritual discernment, the more familiar I was in hearing the Holy Spirit's voice. All of this was new to me so I had no idea how to articulate what was happening to me internally. I had no one to help me through this transition. Never knowing that God had been with me the entire time. I was never alone because I had Him.

I had no words to describe these newfound experiences. God had isolated me in this cocoon stage so I could totally lean on Him as He worked on my transformation. The more I sat in classes and services and prayed, the more God became real to me. We all go through a cocoon period at some point in our life when we are being used by God. Don't fight it, embrace it and allow God to transform you into a beautiful butterfly for His glory.

I cannot say that I have ever heard God's voice. Imagining someone so mighty, so great would have such a large voice, even thunderous maybe, I may not be able to absorb such a sound. But, I can say that I have heard the Holy Spirit speaking to me.

> *"Then He said, 'Go out, and stand on the mountain before the Lord.' And behold, the Lord passed by, and a great and strong wind tore into the mountains and broke the rocks in pieces before the Lord, but the Lord was not in the wind; and after the wind an earthquake, but the Lord was not in the earthquake; and after the earthquake a fire, but the Lord was not in the fire; and after the fire* **a**

still small voice. *So it was, when Elijah heard it, that he wrapped his face in his mantle and went out and stood in the entrance of the cave. Suddenly a voice came to him ..."*
~ 1 KINGS 19:11-13 NKJV

In most cases I do hear a still small voice. I have never heard a boisterous sound but I have heard the whisper. Other times I am compelled to do something an unction, if you will. There is a sense in my spirit when I can feel an impression from Him.

Knowing His Voice

People will ask me all the time, what does His voice sound like, what do you hear, or how do you know it's God's voice? This is where I say again, there has never been a time that I can say that it was God that I heard because for me, and this is just my rationale, that if I heard God's voice it would be so loud that it just might break my eardrums. Which is why I believe He tells the Holy Spirit what to tell us and that is why I say it's the Holy Spirit that has spoken to me. Other people may have heard God's voice but that's not my story. One day I just might and I know there will be no doubt whose voice I have heard in that moment.

To tell you how I know it's the Holy Spirit speaking to me, I can confidently tell you that it's still trial and error every day. The devil doesn't leave us alone simply because we changed sides. He wants nothing more than to see us fail. He tried his best to get me to follow his voice. That's why I had to remain in God's presence as often as I did. Where the Holy Spirit is the devil will not be.

Internal Reconstruction

There are times in this life that I have wanted things so badly that I didn't wait on the Lord to answer. I would say that I "heard" Him say it, but quite often when it didn't turn out the way that God would have had it turn out, then that's when I knew it wasn't the Holy Spirit speaking to me. I call this my trial and error phase.

One book that I read on discernment was *Spiritual Discernment* by Watchman Nee. In it he says that we have to have a spirit-controlled soul. He says there are three steps to this: "The first step is to see the condition of the mind in the light of God. The second step is to drive out or cast aside such unhealthy thoughts. And the third step is to return to quietness in God's presence." He also said that to discern, "we need a workable spirit by which to diagnose another's spirit."

It is important for me to stay in God's presence to know His will and His way, so I am hearing the Holy Spirit's voice as He guides me, as God gives Him what to say to me.

> *"Now He who searches the hearts knows what the mind of the Spirit is, because He makes intercession for the saints according to the will of God."*
> ~ ROMANS 8:27 NKJV.

Each person is different. Each situation is unique. Stress, anxiety, nerves—it all can make you think you are hearing from the Holy Spirit. These emotions are not of God. We have to have Godly thoughts, the mind of Christ. I had a "workable spirit," a teachable spirit. I was ready to cast aside the thoughts that were not of God. That was my biggest trial to overcome.

Learning to hear the Holy Spirit's (God's) voice, to distinguish His voice from any other, is no different than a child knowing their parents' voice. Perhaps it could be the voice of a significant other, someone that you are in a meaningful relationship with.

When you enter into a relationship, you spend time in their presence. Their voice becomes so familiar to you, that you can be standing in a crowded room and hear their voice succinctly. There's no doubt because you've spent time with them. If you are in doubt as to whether or not it's their voice, it's because you didn't spend quality time with them. This is the same when learning to hear the voice of the Holy Spirit.

Get alone with God on a regular, consistent basis, not only when you are in need. Schedule time with Him on your calendar. Turn the television off. Put the phone away. Step away from all of your devices. Practice. Practice. Practice.

Foundations

For me it was whose voice was I hearing? The devil had a field day with that one when it came to me hearing the Holy Spirit. His best weapon against me was doubt. I was questioning if it was the Holy Spirit that I was really hearing. It took years before I completely let go of that spirit of fear and doubt. I continued reading, praying, and staying in His presence. There is nothing too hard for God. I came pretty close to giving Him something too hard, but even my life wasn't something He couldn't fix. People, hope is readily available. All you have to do is want it.

The one fixation I had when learning about God and having a relationship with Him was the way that Archbishop Bailey (First Cathedral) always made it a point to pray. I would see him at the 6:00 a.m. prayer services sitting down against the wall with Mrs. Bailey, having a quiet conversation with God. They weren't up yelling and screaming, or running around, but they were quietly sitting down, having a gentle conversation with God.

Archbishop Bailey was at every prayer service that I ever went to. I modeled my prayer life after his. It was just great seeing another model of prayer from a man in a position of authority like him. He would humble before God and to go to Him in prayer. If he wasn't praying, then he was teaching us about prayer. He taught us how to enter into the throne room of God.

This was the foundation that God knew I needed for where I was headed and what I would have to go through to get to my divine destiny. I would not have made it this far without the power of prayer and the presence of the Almighty God.

> *I would not have made it this far without the power of prayer and the presence of the Almighty God.*

I have had many encounters with the Holy Spirit, whether in dreams, in visions, or directing me through the Bible. A couple of incidents in particular I can remember as if it were yesterday.

While living here in Ohio, I was attending a church service at my church, The Worship Center, and it was high praise in the place. A prophet of God was laying hands on people as he had us go up around the altar for prayer. He laid hands on me, and I fell out in the spirit. When I came to, I went back to my seat and then started to pray in tongues. I could still see people were walking around. Some were praising and some were praying while I was in my seat with no one else around.

I then saw in a vision an octopus with all eight of it's tentacles (arms). The Holy Spirit told me that I was seeing eight generational curses that were on my immediate family from centuries before us. He told me that I was standing in the gap at that time to destroy them from my immediate family, and for the generations to come. It wasn't going to happen overnight but it was the start. He listed the eight out for me, and I've been in prayer over them ever since. I have seen most of them destroyed, but to God be the glory for when all eight will have been destroyed forever.

> *Had I not had a firm foundation in prayer it would have been close to impossible to withstand.*

Had I not had a firm foundation in prayer, it would have been close to impossible to withstand that type of experience. To God be the glory! He is omniscient. I vowed that after all the knowledge and experiences that I had, leading up to the purpose of my creation, that one day I would share with others in hopes of encouraging them to continue to level up. This was evidence that you need to feed your spirit continually.

Daddy's Girl

My first attempt as getting this knowledge out to people was to write my first book almost 12 years ago. I had no outline, no training- nothing to go by other than what I saw in other books. My attempt to write then became so frustrating. It was neither the right time nor the right purpose. I wanted people to share my experiences but not one of growth in the spirit. I thought I could write about my life up to that point but that was not God's plan at the time. It would have been a book on brokenness and bitterness without a remedy. This was just before I received the prophetic word from God about going into photography.

The book was never written. I only succeeded at giving it a title. *Daddy's Girl,* from the aspect of "Daddy" being my Heavenly Father. That idea for the book ignited thoughts of my life and being a "daddy's girl," something I never was. I started to hear the song by Luther Vandross, *Dance with My Father Again*. The lyrics were:

> *"Back when I was a child, before life removed all the innocence, my father would lift me high and dance with my mother and me, and then spin me around 'til I fell asleep. Then up the stairs he would carry*

me, and I knew for sure I was loved, if I could get another chance, another walk, another dance with him, I'd play a song that would never ever end, how I'd love, love, love to dance with my father again."

I thought about the movies and television shows where little girls danced on their father's feet, as he would dance around the floor holding tightly to their daughter's little hands while they would glide along the floor.

One day while working on this unpublished book I took a break to pray. I headed up to my bedroom for a shower first but then I felt the presence of God and made praying at that moment a priority. I didn't know how long He would stay and I didn't want to take the chance of missing out at that time when I desperately needed His guidance.

Fur Elise

Before having to pack up all of our things and moving them into that storage unit, I had a music box carousel that sat atop my bedroom dresser. For some reason I felt the need to pick it up off the dresser and then sat down on my bedroom floor against the wall to pray while holding the carousel in my hands. As I was well into my prayer a vision appeared before me.

While this vision was playing out before me, I saw myself in a garden, in an array of the most beautiful flowers I had ever seen. The garden seemed to go on forever. I was dressed in a fancy purple dress; I was in a dress that made me feel like a princess. I danced around to Fur Elise as I heard it softly playing in the vision. As the vision continued, I began to twirl around what appeared to be like a tree trunk that had suddenly appeared in this vision. As I continued to twirl and dance, I noticed that the tree trunk started to look like a finger. The "prints" on this trunk were actually fingerprints on this gigantic finger I was now dancing with, as the vision continued.

I began to glide along, and then I saw off to the side what appeared to be a throne. There were two king sized chairs with this yellowish gold light beaming from behind. The chair on the left was empty. The chair on the right had a man sitting on it, wearing a white robe. His skin was copper in color. He had dark, wooly hair. When I glanced at him I could see that He was sitting back in the chair with a smile on His face. At times a soft, quiet chuckle would come from this man sitting on the throne in this vision.

Then, the music stopped. The dance ended as I curtsied to thank the person that this enormous finger belonged to. In a very deep, gentle whisper I heard in my ear as I bowed, *"My favorite color is purple."* Then at that very moment, I knew I was dancing with my Father, my heavenly Father. There is nothing like being in the presence of God.

I never saw any other parts of God's body. The finger came from out of the sky, which tells me He is just that big a God. I never saw His face. I only saw part of His finger, the tip that was the size of a tree. Then I knew the empty chair on the left was God's. That meant the Man that I saw in the chair on the right was Jesus.

While still sitting on the floor, I realized I was still holding the carousel in my hands and decided to wind it up to hear the music, while thinking about the vision I just saw. When the music began to play, it softly played… none other than… Fur Elise by Beethoven. Some people may think this was coincidental and that's their prerogative. For me, it was a reassurance that God has always been with me.

> *For me it was a reassurance that God has always been with me.*

Internal Reconstruction

What a life changing experience, to have danced with my heavenly Father. To learn something so personal about God, that He has a favorite color, purple. Purple symbolizes "royalty."

> *"Then Jesus came out, wearing the crown of thorns and the purple robe. And Pilate said to them, 'Behold the Man'!"*
> - JOHN 19:5 NKJV

I sat on that bedroom floor for quite some time, unable to move, not wanting to leave His presence. The peace that came over me has never been forgotten. What a wonderful spiritual moment I experienced on that day. The internal reconstruction finally took place.

Then, in a whisper, I heard, *"You have carried around the burden long enough of not having a college degree. Because of your obedience you will receive your reward, in the land of the living."* He repeated, *"The door for you to go to college was closed by Me. With all that I am going to do, those that will see it will see My glory. You did not know it but you have attended the school of the Holy Spirit and you have obtained your Ph.D, Prophetic, Healing, and Deliverance in Me."*

There was nothing more I needed to say about ever going to get a college degree. Who can argue with that rationale? These past years of getting myself together, learning so much about the Who behind the why, I've been studying all along and have obtained my Ph.D in God.

That was the moment with God that I needed for my physical and spiritual transformation to take place. My internal reconstruction was well on its way after having danced with my heavenly Father.

God cares about every fiber of our being. He knows our hearts, our cares, and our worries. He knows what scares us and what has hurt us. He knows where we lack and what we desire.

> *"But the very hairs of your head are all numbered. Do not fear therefore; you are of more value than many sparrows."*
> – LUKE 12:7 NJKV

He wants us to remain connected to Him so our experiences with Him can take us to another level in our lives that we can't even imagine. I am a living witness that God can take a mess and turn it around from the inside out! Yes, I know I've been changed.

We have to want to be in His presence. He is there waiting on us to arrive. When we purposefully make time for God, He will make memories with us. He will give us visions and experiences that men would be envious of. He will show us things in the heavenly realm that many people can't, and won't experience. We should always want to improve our spiritual, physical, and emotional beings. We need to build our strength to overcome every obstacle that tries to block our way. We tend to ask God to remove our burdens, but He is telling us that as we are carrying them it's making us stronger. There will come a time when we are working out our muscles, spiritually and physically, that if we stay at it long enough and change to healthy eating, the "fat" will eventually fall off. We have to keep at it. The "fat," (the burdens) are falling off. Keep flexing.

The physical and emotional reconstruction must begin with forgiveness.

> *"Therefore, as the elect of God, holy and beloved, put on tender mercies, kindness, humility, meekness, longsuffering; bearing with one another, and forgiving one another, if anyone has a complaint against another; even as Christ forgave you, so you also must do."*
> – COLOSSIANS 3:12-13 NJKV

If we harbor unforgiveness and hold grudges, that brings about an unhealthy lifestyle. It creates blood pressure to rise, along with worry and stress. It causes us to make bad food choices and then gain unnecessary weight. This is not the life that God has purposed for us. We keep ourselves in bondages that He sent His Son to destroy. It's not meant for us to pick back up the bondages that Jesus came to destroy. The life that God has designed for you and I to live, is one of good health, and that includes forgiveness. I learned to forgive myself of some of the bad choices I made as a child, a long time ago, in my years as a child. When I freed myself from unforgiveness, I was able to move on in my own life, and that also freed me from the opinions of others.

> *We keep ourselves in bondages that Jesus came to destroy.*

Don't allow yourself or others to keep you bound up in your past and things that God has already forgiven us for. It's the enemy's desire to keep us bound. He doesn't want us to live a life free and prosperous. In order to walk into our divine destiny, we first need to let go of the hate, bitterness, envy and strife. Let it go! It's only going to keep holding you back. It's time to set yourself free. It's time to learn something personal about God that no one else knows. Get in His presence. He wants to share something personal with you that will change your life. He did it for me and He can do the same for you.

Accepting NO Limits

Chapter Four
Re-Alignment

The Difficult Path: *Linethiboth*

"Stand in the ways and see, and ask for the old paths, where the good way is, and walk in it; then you will find rest for your souls. But they said, 'We will not walk in it.'"
~ JEREMIAH 6:16 NKJV

"You will show me the path of life; in Your presence is fullness of joy; at Your right hand are pleasures forevermore."
~ PSALM 16:11 NKJV

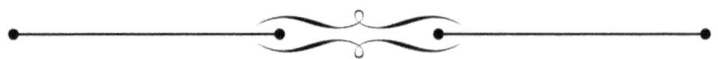

Since receiving the prophetic word in 2006, four years have passed. After having to live with the other families, I finally moved into my own place. After receiving that word along with the dreams I ever had for my future, never did I imagine years would pass and no signs of manifestation. To keep from losing hope or my focus, daily I would encourage myself in the Word or in song and at times had many high hopes that my time had come. Every morning I would say, "Surely today is the day." Yet, night after night, month after month, still nothing.

In order to live in the now I gave God thanks for the "manna," the blessings that kept me encouraged, along the way. One of those blessings was that we were no longer in a basement of a friend's house, or in a spare room with our possessions in those five black trash bags. My hope was that each morning when I awoke it brought me one day closer to His promises. Each day it gave me another opportunity to work out the process of building my business but I missed so much because my heart was yearning for the prize. My sight was out of focus.

Though the vision may come from God that doesn't mean we will arrive at it perfectly. We will make the wrong decisions. We will delay the process with our doubt and frustrations. If we focus on the end and not what's in between, we miss the now. The vision is yet for an appointed time. We tend to get ahead of God instead of staying in pace with God. The excitement builds up from the vision, and gets smoldered through the process because we are out of alignment with God's order.

Looking back, considering the state of mind in which I was in, barely making enough income, not living in the big house, yet, just enough clothes to fit in the five black trash bags, and not having the business fully functioning, I overlooked the process. My focus was on the promise while hoping and praying for God to get me out of my misery immediately.

I'm not quite certain how I thought God was going to do it. I kept thinking and hoping it was an overnight windfall that just appeared in my life. After all it was such a great promise that it needed great funding. When days and nights came and went and no windfall, I wondered if it was something I was doing or not doing? Each day I continued to speak God's promises over me and I never allowed the dreams to die. I had gone through too much to quit now. I will always be found faithful to God.

Though I didn't see the manifestation happen overnight, God was working out the process behind the scenes. God was using this time to prepare me for what was to come while in my misery. God was using this time to re-align me for His purpose.

I couldn't come out of this with bitterness, anger, envy, and strife. Those characteristics are not of Christ. Those characteristics cannot exist in God's divine purpose for our lives. I had to show compassion, love and forgiveness. This is all part of the cocoon process, the waiting. This is when we are being re-aligned with our Creator.

> *Though I didn't see the manifestation happen overnight, God was working out the process behind the scenes.*

When God brings us through, successfully, it is so He can use our story to bring glory to Himself for the purpose of drawing others to Him. Joseph's dream came to pass when he governed like it was shown to him. His family eventually went to him to keep from starving and was reunited with him. Joseph would have missed God's glory, had he not let go of the bitterness and resentment towards his brothers. Instead, he showed love and compassion. It's time to let it go.

Re-Alignment

Every waking moment I was focused on the promise and missing how God was taking me through and re-aligning me. That manna can be taken for granted. It can be overlooked and under appreciated and we rob God of the praise for His provision. This is what is called being ungrateful. Manna served as daily bread for the children of Israel. They couldn't take that day's portion into the next day as it spoiled too quickly. It was meant for that day. There are so many opportunities missed in a day because we think we have tomorrow. God is saying "no," tomorrow is not promised to you. Take advantage of every second to seek Me to know the path that was designed specifically for you.

God didn't have to bring me through the way that He did. It could have been much worse. Some people do end up on the streets. Some people don't have one black trash bag, let alone five. Others may not have friends that would take in an adult, their child and a dog. And then to be allowed access to parts of the house and the use of the car, was truly a blessing. This was all part of the re-alignment; giving me an opportunity to show my gratitude. God is worthy of the praise.

Being on my own meant having to pay for my own rent, utilities, and food again. I had no mode of transportation at this time but that didn't keep me from getting to and from my part-time job on foot. Walking long distances wasn't anything new to me.

As a kid I had to walk to school and back at the same distance that I was now walking as an adult to work. Our parents weren't the ones that took us to and from practice or school. If we wanted to play a sport we had to walk to practice and home. Not one time did they pick us up or drop us off. This helped me into becoming an independent and determined person. I truly believe that this life was given to me because God knew I was strong enough to handle it.

Walking back then as a youth has prepared me for this moment in time, now as an adult. It allowed me more time with God. The encouragement and plans for my life that He shared with me during these times gave me hope.

The owner where I worked was very nice to me. At times he would pick me up or take me home whenever he was available. He always talked to me about getting my own transportation. He didn't know at that time how horrific my credit had become.

Mansion On A Hill

The place where I lived was a new development. I was approved for this brand new unit that still hadn't been completed. With my credit as bad as it was, I knew that it was God who stepped in and put things in place for me in order to get this new place. The one unit I was approved for was still under construction, but I was desperate. How could a new place approve me with the income I was making from a part-time job and the credit I had? I know that it was God that opened this door for me. Without Him there was no way I would have ever been able to be approved on my own.

Every day I would go by to peep in the window to my new place and watch it being built as if it were a mansion on a hill. It was home to me, it was going to be mine and I could have a place for my daughter to live when she was home from school. This place was so new it still didn't have streets paved.

When my unit was available, I signed the lease and picked up the keys and moved in with those five black bags of clothes and shoes and documents that I kept in my possession. No furniture, no dishes, no electronics -just me and my bags, but it was mine. This gave me hope. This gave me the determination to live the dream that God spoke into my life.

Those early mornings when I would get up to walk to work, the construction workers were already there building the units next to me. In the afternoon the same workers were there and said they would look out for me while the construction was going on. At this point I was depending on friends to get me to places that were too far to walk because I still didn't have my own car- not for lack of trying, but the expense and the approval just wasn't happening with the one job.

Eventually, someone from the job gave me a sofa that was barely used. My boss was kind enough to assist me in getting it to my place. I tried desperately to find another way to get it to my home because I was too embarrassed to have him come in and see how I was living, but there was no one else available to help.

He came and saw the condition and as polite as he was, he never mentioned it to me. He knew I was starting over but with little of what I shared with him about my personal life, he thought I was starting over from my divorce. I was not going to explain to him that I was in this situation because of my faith. It wasn't God that got me into this situation but it was God that kept me while I was in it. My lack of knowledge of getting to my destiny more accurately was what got me into this situation.

I prayed for God to "rescue" me. I prayed for God to get me to the Promised Land. In the way that God was providing the answers, I didn't see it because I was looking at the bigger picture and not necessarily at the how to. I was looking for God to answer in another way, and by missing the way He was answering, I delayed my arrival.

> *I was looking for God to answer in another way by missing the way He was answering I delayed my arrival.*

Shortly after he helped me move the sofa in, he encouraged me to look for transportation. That would be the next thing for me to look into, but for now I had to find a way to earn more income to afford transportation.

Crossroads

Regardless of the circumstances around me not looking like what I believed in my heart that they should, I was not going to let that deter me. Having been given a share of stubbornness and determination, I combined that with my faith in God, there was no stopping me. My situation at the time had in no way lined up with what God promised me about doing just photography, but I was determined to see it through.

In my heart of hearts I knew deep down inside that God was going to do just as He said. "God is not a man, that He should lie. Nor a son of man that He should repent. Has He said and will He not do it? Or has He spoken, and will He not make it good? Behold, I have received a command to bless; He has blessed, and I cannot reverse it." Numbers 23:19-20 NKJV. I had my faith and I had God controlling the entire situation. Jeremiah 6:16 says, *"Stand in the ways and see …"*

In Chaim Bentorah's book *Hebrew Word Study* he writes:

> *"The next thing we are told to do is to "see." This word is ra'ah and is often viewed as a spiritual seeing, as in discernment or as in seeing like a prophet or a seer. In this context, it would appear that one is to try to imagine what lies at the end of each road, or is looking at the consequences of taking each road."*

Over the course of time I have found that when I make the God choice, it brings peace into my decision. If I ever feel uneasy, it's either that I haven't made a choice or I made the easy choice. There's something to choosing the "difficult, hidden path" that God presents to us.

Chaim Bentorah writes:

"But before taking a particular path, we must 'amad (is spelled ayin, mem, daleth. Ayin speaks of God's ominiscience, or all-knowing; mem signifies that God reveals some of this knowledge, which opens a daleth, or a door, to His presence. Hence, what you contemplate is the revealed knowledge of God that will lead you through a doorway to His presence.), or pause, to prayerfully contemplate our journey and make sure we take the right path, the way that is in harmony with God. We must pause to consider our path, because left to ourselves, we will instinctively choose the path of least resistance and not the path that is limethiboth – hidden or uncertain. God's perfect will might be the limethiboth, or the more difficult, hidden, or uncertain path."

> *He reminded me that my purpose is to capture beauty through His eyes. My choice was simple; I had complete trust in God.*

At this current crossroad, do I stand and wait on God to reveal the hidden or uncertain path, or was God presenting the hidden, uncertain path, as the easy path to me? No one ever said the process would be easy. At this point, I have come too far for God to leave me in a worse condition than when I began.

As I continued through the process, God reminded me of the houses He led me to see, the land He instructed me to look for to build my house on. He reminded me that my purpose is to capture beauty through His eyes. My choice was simple; I had complete trust in God.

Journal Entries

Still only having one income from a part-time job, fear of eviction from this new place was ever present. Every month I was anxious of not being able to pay the rent on time. I needed God to intervene for me. I wasn't letting go until He blessed me. They worked with me each month until I was able to pay the rent. I found myself excited for the approaching New Year because that meant it was time to file taxes. Undoubtedly I'd get a refund. This was not the best course of action but it was helping me through my "wilderness" experience.

While scribing this book I came across a journal entry that I made on August 2, 2007 (nine years ago today) at 8:37 a.m., after having been led to read Psalm 92 that morning, here are God's comments to me that I entered that day:

> *"During this time of extreme pressure, do not look at your circumstances. This is the time that the devil will put the most pressure on you to cause you to fear and doubt Me. I want you to fill your mouth with praises to Me. Fill your house with songs to Me. This will cause the devil to be defeated. People are going to know that My hand has been upon you!"*

This entry was made before my time in my new place. I continued to journal and to read over the past journal entries. This kept me encouraged. God had never given up on me and I wasn't going to let a slow going pace cause me to give up on Him.

Here is another from August 15, 2007 at 8:12 a.m., after having been led to read Jonah 1:17, here are God's comments to me that I entered that day:

> *"You are in a holding pattern. There is absolutely nothing you can do to fix this. I have made you to stand still and see the salvation of Me. You have done well with all that has come your way. As I did with My servant Jonah and made him still for three days, there wasn't a thing he could do except wait on Me. I have a purpose and a plan for you. In this time of waiting, pray, praise, and rejoice. I am on your side and*

that will be evident in the days to come! Rejoice for the heavens are rejoicing with you."

Though these entries were made years before, they are still relevant to me now. No matter what I would try, if God closes a door there is nothing getting through it. Though it was slow going I still had to depend and wait on the Lord.

Every time I turned around God was providing just enough to get me through and it caused me to totally depend on Him.

Humble Interview

I was in between figuring out how to market my photography at least, get the clients in so I could do this full-time. Since that wasn't happening for me, at the time I had to find employment to sustain my new normal. If I had to work a job, to fund my dream job then why not start with something in the same field of photography? That was my "light bulb" moment, my "a-ha" moment. How many years could I have shaved off had I gone this route the first time?!

One day in 2008, I saw an article in the "want ads" online for a receptionist position at a photography studio, and I was beyond excited. I recognized it as an opportunity for me, an opened door that God was placing in front of me, to lead me into my divine destiny. I could have let my pride get the better of me, applying for a receptionist position; after all, I was in my forties and to me I should be further along in my career than this. Thankfully God doesn't see us how we see ourselves. Though it was a receptionist position, it would be in a photography studio. If I had to clean toilets to be closer to my purpose I'd do it.

Putting my pride aside, I dressed professionally for the job interview as if it were a once in a lifetime opportunity. I was nervous at the interview because I wasn't a "professional" photographer. What if I didn't qualify to work in a studio, even as a receptionist? Then a calm came over me and I remembered Whose I was.

The interview took place and I was offered the position and I accepted. In the back of my mind I knew being a receptionist at the studio was a stepping-stone, I had God's promises after all. It wouldn't be long before I would see them manifest, or so I thought. Either way, I had a job in a photography studio and I never lost hope.

This job was only part-time and with the other part-time job they barely gave me the income I needed to keep the lights on and food on the table. Yet I still held on to my promises from God. I had hope in Him. This is what He told me to do, just photography. I was on the path in which He placed me. I had to keep my focus on Him.

> *I was on the path in which He placed me. I had to keep my focus on Him.*

I worked that job with passion and gratitude because I knew that God was working out His promises and plans for me. I knew my beginning was not my end. And here is where the manna was being provided. I stopped focusing on the bigger picture and began to trust God in the process. Four years earlier I could have taken this route but my judgment was clouded. My determination was aimed in the wrong direction.

I Am A Photographer

I learned as much as I could about the business and started establishing relationships with the staff and the clients that would come in as "regulars." This helped me in re-aligning my business plan as a photographer. I started helping out in the photo sessions with prepping and staging. One day after an opportunity to photograph a practice session, my manager reviewed my proofs. She called me over to discuss them and to give her feedback on them. She showed me areas where I could change some things. She complimented me and asked, "You're a photograph aren't you?"

Racing through my mind was doubt about being a professional photographer. According to a business definition of "professional," no, I was not a "professional" photographer. I have the love and passion for taking pictures, I see the end result in my mind and try to capture that image. In my heart of hearts I was a photographer, just not a "professional" one. I never had the educational background that warranted me being a "professional" photographer. No degree in the subject or the credentials that come along with saying that one is a "professional."

You see, she never asked me if I was a professional photographer. All along that was doubt that crept in and tried to talk me out of my honest response. She saw something in me that I never said audibly to anyone, not even to myself. She saw a natural talent, an eye for photography. I had people skills and could draw the best out of them, especially to capture it on "film." That day I pushed doubt aside and with confidence I replied to her, "Yes, I am a photographer!" Yes, I said it audibly. What a relief. Yes, I am a photographer. No college degree but natural ability. College couldn't teach Lebron James how to be a professional basketball player. By design he was a basketball player. He just needed the opportunity in that arena.

As I think back, I realize that God was perfecting this craft in me as a photographer, as He had given me years to practice on my own. Slowly crawling along in my caterpillar stage in life. Unknowingly, He became my instructor, unknowingly. Guiding me. Teaching me. Protecting me. He blessed me along the way with a personal model, my daughter. This gave me years of practice to pose her with trying out different outfits and ideas. Long before I knew what my purpose was I was working out the process.

From the time she was born, I always had a camera in her face. That worked until she started getting older. I noticed the resentment from her towards my "hobby" and I lost my model, or so I thought. What must have seemed like torment to her, she began to turn away from my camera, but one day she began to come around in her teen years. No matter what mood she was in, no matter if I caught her in the middle of eating, texting or doing homework, I managed to get that million-dollar smile. I think she finally realized that maybe if I smile, she'll just go away.

When it came to photography I had no formal training. It was all self-taught. Anything and everything I knew about taking pictures I learned from experience along the way. With experience and books on the subject matters of photography, faith, spiritual growth, finances, I became what God purposed for me all along.

If we allow Him, the Holy Spirit is an amazing teacher and business partner. He was sent to comfort us. Too many times we ignore Him and we end up working much harder for things that would come so naturally to us.

If we allow Him, the Holy Spirit is an amazing teacher and business partner.

Things were beginning to align themselves. One day at the studio I was put on the floor for my first "professional" photo session. It was much harder being a lead photographer than an assistant. But that wasn't going to stop me. Studio photography is much different than anything taken anywhere else.

I started asking friends to come into the studio for free sessions so I could practice. I eventually took the certification course and passed. Since I was going to do this professionally, I needed to add to my base of knowledge and skills and find new ways of positioning people in unexpected situations. Capturing a crying baby doesn't always appeal to the masses. I had to find ways around situations that presented themselves in a session.

God had placed me in a pool of talented photographers to learn from, while getting paid to do what I love, that's manna. That's where I learned that great photos couldn't be forced. There are times that you just have to try another day and that's okay.

Time went on and more opportunities and training came along during my days, months, and years at the studio, I was grateful for the opportunities that were given to me while working there. I stayed with the photo studio and became a certified (professionally trained in posing, lighting, and correct ways to capture portraitures) photographer. I was making good use of my time while waiting on God's manifestation.

Three years after I began as a receptionist I worked my way into becoming a "professional" photographer. After all these years and making my way as a professional, an increase in pay was bound to come my way. Maybe even a full-time position?

Daily Manna

I worked these two part-time jobs to build up enough to maintain my new place. No car, no furniture, no dishes, no t.v. but it was mine. Alyssa now had another place in Ohio to call home. By it being a brand new development I was one of the first to move in while they were still building the rest around me. I always went to sleep each night believing that God was letting me know that He was building a strong foundation for me and the walls going up around me would never be able to come down again.

Each day I would get up thanking Him in anticipation for the Promised Land manifestation. Yet, each day I would go to "bed" (actually lying on the floor) realizing that that moment hadn't arrived. I still had God's spoken word but no evidence.

I would find ways to encourage myself by consistently attending Bible Study and Sunday worship. I would always find ways to play Gospel music to keep from going crazy. I had the Holy Spirit that would never leave me nor forsake me. Daily I had to encourage myself in the Lord to keep moving. I had the word of God and I had the daily dose of manna that He would provide.

> *Daily I had to encourage myself in the Lord to keep moving, my daily dose of manna.*

Two part-time jobs just made up enough to get by, not to get ahead. But things picked up at the studio and so did my hours. I didn't have time to work at the graphic design store so by faith I let that job go. Things once again began to look prosperous. Then the economy took a turn, and so did the hours at the photo studio. God, why couldn't this be a simpler journey?

During this time of figuring out God's plans for my life and having my hours cut back at the studio, I received an eviction notice on my apartment door. Desperation kicked in. I prayed and cried and prayed and cried. Wanting to keep my faith in tact, I did more praying than crying. God soon provided a *daleth* (an open door). The day before the eviction would have happened, I was approved for another apartment just across the street from the development I was being evicted from. Though I was leaving this new apartment development, I was still accountable for the remaining rent owed for the duration of the lease. That was the least of my concerns at the time; I had to get out of there before I was thrown out.

The hours at the studio began to pick back up again. Being led by God, I began making progress. I went to a dealership that, helped people with bad credit to improve their credit. It was a struggle because with places like that, they charge more than an average auto dealership would. I was approved and chose a Dodge Caravan-the pickings were very slim at this lot. I was proud of my minivan. I had no younger children to justify the purchase, but I was no longer walking to work or the grocery store. I was no longer depending on others for rides.

I did my best to make the weekly payments, going out of my way to drop off the payments, weekly, because they couldn't be mailed. I was at their mercy until my credit made a comeback and God has a way of humbling His children. With God's help I was getting things back in place. No longer asking for rides to work was a blessing. Paying for the car and rent was now another issue.

The day I had to move there was no one available to help me. I managed to move all of my things using my new van that I became the proud owner of and hauled everything just across the street. The dishes I managed to purchase were all packed up and ready to go. Out with the old and into the new.

I eventually had to get another job to help cover the expenses of my apartment and a car. Things were starting to come together. My home was still unfurnished minus a daybed that was given to me, as well as a few dishes here and there.

I managed to find a temporary job as a customer service rep for an education publishing company a couple of months before I moved into this new apartment. No, the temporary job wasn't photography but I was living in my now, trusting God and not losing sight of the manna.

Things started to look brighter for me. My wait must be over, after all I have my own place, I have a working vehicle, I have a full-time, temporary job, and still working part-time in the studio, this must be where my wait ends, or does it?

Re-Alignment

I had to start making connections but wasn't sure which direction to go. During the time that I was out of work, while the Holy Spirit was leading me on how to build my photography business, I was finding places to order business cards. I was getting accounts set up and making connections with people to establish a clientele. Working this angle of having my own photography business, I needed it to work out simultaneously with an actual paying job in order to keep a roof over our heads. Now was not the time to go backwards.

I had to believe that whatever decision I made at this point about a full-time job outside of photography to sustain myself that He would work it out for my good and His glory. One path or the other wouldn't take me off course, they both were God's way but I had to make a decision either, to work the full-time temporary job only or to hang on to both and not have time to advance my own photography business?

I had to stop beating myself up with the guilt of feeling like I would let God down if I hadn't stayed within the photography field. I had to rid myself of this guilt because when He instructed me to do photography He never said I would be working for anyone else as a photographer. Working for someone else within this field would afford me the opportunity to gain more experience and to see how to run my own business. That didn't mean to work for them always.

When I let go of the guilt the burden was released and I was free to walk into my purpose. I was re-aligned to begin living in my purpose. I knew then that it was time to let some things go.

> *When I let go of the guilt the burden was released and I was free to walk in my purpose.*

The temporary seasonal position was over but they extended my contract out in another department, this was the call-center. Still not a permanent position nor an increase in pay the expenses continued to add up. The reality was these expenses were simply the cost of living. But when you are receiving close to minimum wage as a temp, it seemed close to impossible to maintain my current cost of living. I had peace about my decision to move and to take on this temporary full-time job so it was time to see where this path was going to take me.

Backward Steps

With one door closing there was going to be another door opening. I knew that I wasn't brought out of bondage only to die in my wilderness experience. This may have been too much for someone else to survive but this was my story, my life, and I was determined to see it through. I kept my sights on my destiny and that kept me hopeful. "I will live and not die" I kept telling myself.

With the certification in photography and all the experiences I gained on running a photography business, with deep sorrow, I turned in my resignation at the photo studio. Having to leave behind so many amazing people, both with the staff and the customers, it was a hard decision to make. But a closed door is a closed door. It was time for me to move on. I didn't let go of the friends I made at this studio. Somewhere down the road our paths would cross again.

Working this temporary position felt like I was taking steps backwards instead of moving forward in terms of my career. Where I started as a temp, it felt as if I was starting over in my career. This was part of the process to be re-aligned. I chose humility over pride. The pay was starting wage. The position was one I would have taken out of high school. God was certainly humbling me.

The struggle was real. Even in the new place I was behind on my rent due to the wages I was receiving. Each day I would come home from work, I would walk up the pathway to my front door. Sweating and nervous about what I might see on my door, I would walk slowly to the door and peep around the wall, as if that would make a potential notice of late payment or a promise to leave the premises go away.

This became a daily habit that I still do today for no reason at all. The anxiety and dread I felt each day I would return home. The enemy did his best to get me to abort God's promises through these tactics. The struggle of getting things back in place was real. Something else I needed to be delivered from.

Three months into the new place I received word that my temporary assignment was going to end that week. I placed all my eggs into this one basket. Why was this happening to me again? Why was I faced with another chance to lose everything after just getting back on my feet? God, why was this my life? None of this looked like what He showed me in the dreams. None of it matched up to any of the prophetic words that had ever been spoken into my life about prosperity. I started to doubt myself at times, was this just a figment of my imagination, something I made up? All I know is this emotional rollercoaster was making me nauseous.

Here is a journal entry from October 5, 2010 at 7:34 p.m.:

> *"Truly, this is a setup of ALL setups! I am stunned, I feel numb but some how I am digging deep down in my soul to find an ounce of faith, a glimpse of hope! Today I was given the news that my assignment as a temp will end this Friday! I have sickness in my body; the issue of blood won't stop. I believe a cyst was found on my rib cavity and I have an eviction notice that I may have to contend with! BUT GOD! I am praying for Your guidance in this and that I don't get anxious and move ahead of You! Show me a way to walk into my prosperity! I am trusting You God!" Signed, "Your daughter."*

What was I to do? If I panicked it would not have resolved anything. Just as quickly as doubt and fear crept in, I remembered that God told me to replace it with praise. I found some praise music and began to praise my way through. What? How could I praise at a time like this? I did because that felt right to me during this trial.

I turned my fear into praise. I turned my mourning into dancing. I refused to let doubt win. Remembering Whose I was, I knew God wouldn't set me up for failure. If I had to lose it I knew God had another path in store for me, one that would lead me to my victory. I praised Him that day like a little kid on Christmas morning. It was an opportunity for my praise to confuse the enemy.

> *I turned my fear into praise, my mourning into dancing, I refused to let doubt win.*

No, my praise didn't change the outcome that day but I certainly felt inspired and confident that God was not going to let me down. The assignment ended without anything in place. I didn't allow worry or doubt to enter back into my spirit.

Mourning Into Dancing

I enjoyed the few days off and used that time to focus on God and to listen as He instructed me during this time. God has a history of providing a ram in the bush. In the Bible, God instructed Abraham to sacrifice his son, the one that was promised to him. He took the lad up to be sacrificed and here is where we find God stepping in:

> *"But the Angel of the Lord called to him from heaven and said, 'Abraham, Abraham!' And he said, 'Here I am.' And He said, 'Do not lay your hand on the lad, or do anything to him; for now I know that you fear*

God, since you have not withheld your son, your only son, from Me.' Then Abraham lifted his eyes and looked, and there behind him was a ram caught in a thicket by its horns. So Abraham went and took the ram, and offered it up for a burnt offering instead of his son."
~ GENESIS 22:11-14 NKJV

Just as I was willing to sacrifice my new beginnings to continue trusting in God here comes the ram in the bush. My phone rang and I had a new assignment, with the same company but with better hours, a better location, and a slight increase in pay. Though my praise didn't change the outcome immediately, it did get me through that week of dark days and sleepless nights.

My praise turned my mourning into dancing. One door shut and another one opened on my behalf. Faith will move mountains. Fear and doubt will cause mountains to appear. It's time to speak boldly to those mountains and tell them to move. Mountain, you have to move. Get up out of my way. Our words have power. Choose wisely the words you speak into your life.

My praise and my faith aligned with God's promises kept me from going insane. There were times that I wanted to throw in the towel, and just go back to what I considered to be my "norm." Sometimes God is calling us to make the decision to follow Him on the difficult path, the hidden uncertain path, to test our faith. In keeping in harmony with God, it may require us to lose some friends, family and possessions, but God is omniscient, He is all knowing. Because He told me what my future would be, if I hold on and trust in Him, it will be better than I could ever imagine. This was just the beginning.

These were not my easiest days. Getting through these dark times kept me close to God. I kept praise on my lips and remembered our "dance." Because of special moments like those with God, I didn't allow anyone to talk me out of my purpose and destiny that God had for me. I kept the faith and cursed the doubt. These circumstances compelled me to be stronger, to find strength through prayer and praise.

The new assignment was only for a week but I took it anyway. Eventually that one-week turned into a permanent full-time position, and did not require me to work a second job. I was faced with a mountain of debt but I managed to keep the van paid up and a roof over my head. This time around I didn't have to lose it all. I now had to figure out how to get out of the mountain of debt, and continue to be a good steward to be found faithful for more.

I am grateful that God surrounded my daughter and I with some amazing people who stood by us in our "wilderness." With things now re-aligned it's time to see what was in store for us. The future had begun to look a little brighter.

Chapter Five
Recovering

This, Too, Shall Pass: *Gam Zah Yovur*

> "So David inquired of the Lord, saying, '"Shall I pursue this troop? Shall I overtake them?"' And He answered him, '"Pursue, for you shall surely overtake them and without fail recover all."
> - 1 SAMUEL 30:8

> "And He changes the times and the seasons; He removes kings and raises up kings; He gives wisdom to the wise and knowledge to those who have understanding."
> - DANIEL 2:21

I didn't understand then how important journaling could be. Had I not disciplined myself in doing this, I'd have no point of reference and no history recorded. Most of what I am going to share of my entries are reminders for me about how far I've really come. My circumstances caused me to be ungrateful of the smaller victories along the way. I allowed disappointment and frustration to rule.

If we don't stop to thank God, daily, for the smaller victories, we are robbing Him of His glory. Don't be like the devil and not glorify God. If I can leave this little nugget with you… journal and praise God along the journey.

Here are more journal entries I came across as God was taking me along this journey to recover it all.

September 28, 2009 at 8:50 a.m.:

> "Yesterday we were instructed by the Holy Spirit to take an inventory of all the things we lost while trusting in You for the things You promised that You would do! Here is my list: TITHES, peace, joy, love, home, finances, car, clothes, computers, T.V.s, furniture, dishes, vets, dog grooming, shoes, books, Bibles, photos, artwork, papers for Alyssa, memories documented, health insurance, dental insurance, retirement money, stocks, eating out, food shopping, dry cleaning, car wash, hair salon, nail salon, gifts for others, cards for others, (see photos of the move out). Getting it all back and then some!"

I had to say goodbye to life as I knew it, only to say hello to the unknown.

Having lost nearly all of our possessions I felt as though my life as I knew it had been shattered into a thousand pieces. Everything we owned was gone. I had to say good-bye to life as I knew it, only to say hello to the unknown.

This moment brought about anger and fear all mixed into one. It wasn't only me going through this walk of faith; I was taking my daughter along with me. I never gave it one thought of what it could have been doing to her, if it made her mad at God or at me for losing everything. She didn't ask for any of this, she merely was born into a life of a very strong, believing mother. I recall one day driving to church in a borrowed car, asking God, "who would want to serve a poor God?" Who would believe me about serving a God who has everything yet I was not living what I was sharing. He quickly responded, *"I don't want poor children."* This fueled my determination to see God's promises through.

Eventually, I stopped beating myself up for having dragged her down this faith path with me. Giving her up was never an option so she had to go through it with me. I wanted her to witness God in my life. I wanted to give her an opportunity to be a strong woman of God as well. What better example than to show her that trusting God in every situation would produce fruit. My faith was so strong in God, that I knew one day it was all going to be just as He said. Had I thought otherwise, I would have never taken us down this road. And now, on our road to recovery, it's time for the world to see what I had been hearing all along!

When God speaks I've learned to move immediately because I never know how long that door of opportunity will remain open. He who hesitates long, hesitates wrong. It's like when we hear our parents tell us to do something, and if we don't do it we suffer the consequences; at least with my parents that was the result of not responding immediately.

There are times during this walk with God, that He will ask us to do some of the most difficult things to challenge our faith. Believe it or not, it is a trust factor. How much can God trust us with? Do we love our family and things more than we love Him? Are we willing to let go of the things and people we hold so tightly to, out of obedience to Him? He won't leave us broken. He only wants to take us to a better place than where we first said, "yes" to His will. This walk is not for the weak. It is not for everyone, nor will everyone that receives His Son as their personal savior have to go through such trials. Our trials are based on our destiny. Think of it as training. Not everyone enlisted in the military makes it through boot camp.

God places a purpose in each of us to contribute to the greater purpose of His creation. When we acknowledge the purpose, He then begins the process of execution. His process at times may go against the life we've established for ourselves. This is why so many people experience career changes along the way.

His Will

Everyone having major surgery goes through a recovery process. This recovery starts strengthening the area that was just operated on. God performs spiritual surgery, if you will, on us when we accept our purpose; soon thereafter the recovery begins.

Putting our trust, hope, and faith in God and not in our family, friends, jobs, and possessions shows God how He can trust us with even greater. For me, there was no doubt in my mind that when I stepped out on this faith adventure that God was going to do just as He said.

By no means did I make it to the "high income" category with my previous jobs. We were living a very comfortable life, one I wouldn't mind having back even now. However, knowing it's only going to be better than "comfortable". I'll wait. I would love to say and have you believe, that all of what we had it was done God's way and living in His perfect will, but that wasn't the case. Hindsight is always 20/20. Knowing what I know now, had I done it God's way from the beginning, perhaps that would have kept me from receiving the bumps and bruises that I got along the way. Now having gone through, it it's my ultimate goal to reach back and help others to avoid as much pain and agony as they possibly can.

No, I didn't know God at a young age, before I chose my career path. But the moment I knew Him was a time I could have inquired of His will for my life. We have to teach that to those who are beginning a relationship with Him. Seek His will IMMEDIATELY after accepting Him into your life. It should be taught to our children at a very young age. If your story is like mine and you weren't raised in a church either, it's never too late to seek God for your purpose. Moses was 70 when he started out in his purpose. Noah was 500 when he started out in his purpose. It's never too late.

Seek His will immediately after accepting Him into your life.

Because I didn't learn this until I was an adult, as a parent I raised Alyssa to seek God in everything. When she was in seventh grade I remember a vivid conversation I was having with her in the kitchen. She asked me what I thought she should be when she grew up? I had my opinion and ideas, but then I quickly remembered I only had a hand in bringing her into this world. I turned and replied to that innocent little girl becoming a beautiful young lady, and told her, "How about you ask God?" I could see from the reaction on her face that she was not expecting that as an answer.

I explained to her that though I appreciated her asking me as her mother, I felt since God was the one that made her that He would be the one to know what He created her to be. "Ask God in prayer tonight and continue to ask Him until you get the answer you are looking for," I told her.

I wanted to prevent her from having to go through life doing what she wanted and not consulting our Maker. I didn't want her to wind up like the 12 Disciples with a career change, after having met Jesus one day on the job. We tend to follow the same career decision-making path as they did.

Save yourself the frustration and seek God for His will for your life. If you are a parent of a school aged child or younger, there is so much in life that we can help them to avoid, if we tell them to go to God and ask Him what His will is for their lives. Most importantly, they need to WAIT on His answer. Teach this to them at a very young age, train up a child. Sometimes we get impatient with God and find ourselves out of sync with Him, then go to Him crying to fix our issues. God wants us to have joy and live an abundant life this side of Heaven.

Looking back over some of my journal entries, I could see the emotional rollercoaster I had myself on while waiting on God. I could see how I was eagerly trying to find answers daily instead of patiently waiting and living in the present. I spent more time trying to find the when, always looking ahead.

Sometimes in our present moments, is when God can work on us the best. If we haven't seen the "when" it's because God is working on us, preparing us in the present. I had to change my focus. I was in such a frustrating, "I'm so over this" state of mind. I would only stay "stuck" in my wilderness experience fixated on my future, had I not endured the process. Learn to appreciate the blessings, daily. What we appreciate appreciates.

More Journal Entries

During the process while I was searching and looking ahead, I was missing what I already had in my hand. What I needed to use as to how I was designed to fulfill my purpose. All of the pieces were there but I overlooked them by not being PRESENT, in my present. I was a professional photographer all along. It was now time to start acting like one. I had to decompress my thinking and that was what released me to forge ahead.

From this experience, I can say it is not an easy thing to wait on God while in a "storm." This was a dark, dreary, lingering storm. With funnel clouds and harsh winds. Saying I will wait on the Lord is one thing, doing it is another. Specifically, when waiting can go from days, to weeks, to months, to years. After all, God said it was going to happen, right? Even though the storms don't resemble what He said would be we must learn how to wait on God. The storm is passing over, hallelujah! He may not say exactly when He will show up, but that's the faith part.

Here is another journal entry from October 1, 2009 at 5:50 p.m.:

Found myself at the very end of my rope. I was well beyond hope and saw no end in sight. My entire being was just about to give up. But then I heard God in the Spirit say, "'I am here. Ask Me anything,'" I then grabbed a bottle of anointing oil and liberally anointed my head and my hands and knelt before God in the center of my living room! Just the two of us, with me crying my eyes out.

When I stopped searching for my destiny and lived in my present, taking it one day at a time and not trying to fast-forward, here is what was revealed to me in this next journal entry:

Read Job 28:28 NKJV

"And to man He said, 'Behold, the fear of the Lord, that is wisdom, and to depart from evil is understanding.'"
And here is what I heard in the spirit, "Through this process I have OBTAINED wisdom AND mercy!

The devil thought that I would be destroyed in all of this. He was told not to touch Alyssa in it!"

Read Psalm 28 NJKV

"To You I will cry, O Lord my Rock: do not be silent to me. Lest, if You are silent to me, I become like those who go down to the pit. ²Hear the voice of my supplications when I cry to You. When I lift up my hands toward Your holy sanctuary. ³Do not take me away with the wicked and with the workers of iniquity, who speak peace to their neighbors, but evil is in their hearts. ⁴Give to them according to their deeds, and according to the wickedness of their endeavors, give to them according to the works of their hands; render to them what they deserve. ⁵Because they do not regard the works of the Lord, nor the operation of His hands, He shall destroy them and not build them up. ⁶Blessed be the Lord, because He has heard the voice of my supplication! ⁷The Lord is my strength and my shield; my heart trusted in Him, and I am helped; therefore my heart greatly rejoices, and with my song I will praise Him. ⁸The Lord is their strength, and He is the saving refuge of His anointed. ⁹Save Your people and bless Your inheritance; shepherd them also, and bear them up forever."

God has heard my cry! He has opened the windows of heaven. "Don't be afraid, your change is coming!"

Read Psalm 82 NKJV

"God stands in the congregation of the mighty; He judges among the gods. ²How long will you judge unjustly,

and show partiality to the wicked? Selah ³Defend the poor and fatherless; do justice to the afflicted and needy. ⁴Deliver the poor and needy; free them from the hand of the wicked. ⁵They do not know, nor do they understand; they walk about in darkness; all the foundations of the earth are unstable. ⁶I said, "You are gods, and all of you are children of the Most High. ⁷But you shall die like men, and fall like one of the princess.'" ⁸Arise, O God, judge the earth; for You shall inherit all nations."

What I heard in the spirit: "All of the nations will know that I AM! I Am bringing honor back to My name." "Rikki, it is bigger than you, I had to know that I could trust you. Your cries, your petitions have reached My ears. No more sorrow. No more sadness. You are surrounded by nothing and hopelessness but you still praise Me!"

Read Psalm 92 NKJV

"It is good to give thanks to the Lord, and to sing praises to Your name, O Most High; ²to declare Your lovingkindness in the morning, and Your faithfulness every night, ³on an instrument of ten strings, on the lute, and on the harp, with harmonious sound, ⁴for You, Lord, have made me glad through Your work; I will triumph in the works of Your hands. ⁵O Lord, how great are Your works! Your thoughts are very deep, ⁶a senseless man does not know, nor does a fool understand this. ⁷When the wicked spring up like grass, and when all the workers of iniquity flourish, it is that they may be destroyed forever. ⁸But You, Lord, are on high forevermore. ⁹For behold, Your enemies O Lord, for behold, Your enemies shall perish; all the workers of iniquity shall be scattered. ¹⁰But my horn You have exalted *like a wild ox; I have been anointed with fresh oil. ⁱⁱMy eye also has seen my desire on my enemies; my ears hear my desire on the wicked who rise up against me. ¹²The righteous shall flourish like a palm tree, he shall grow like a cedar in Lebanon. ¹³Those who are planted in the house of the Lord shall flourish in the courts of our God, ¹⁴they shall still bear fruit in old age. They shall be fresh and flourishing, ¹⁵to declare that the Lord is upright; He is my rock, and there is no unrighteousness in Him."*

This day I was in a very desperate state! No money for gas, I don't have all of my rent money, which is due TODAY and bill collectors continue to call for old debt. I owe for furniture that I no longer have, I was simply at my very end! All of my hope was gone! <u>*But God!*</u> *He told me to anoint myself and come and ask of Him because I was in His presence! He was here to hear and answer. God, I pray that this moment will be the turning point for the desperate change and manifestation that I need! Only You can do this!* <u>*ONLY YOU!*</u>

~ RIKKI

That ended my journal entry for that day. I could see how I was hard pressed on every side. I stayed in God's presence during the entire journey. There were times when I felt like giving up, but what was I going to go back to? In the movie *My Fair Lady*, she asks the question, "What is to become of me?" Crying, rejoicing, whining, and dancing, all of my emotions were everywhere. You name it, I was experiencing it. There were days when I didn't feel like praying. There were days that I didn't want to go church. ::Gasp:: Yes, there are times when even the strongest Christians are so beat down, that trying to get a prayer out is like trying to lift a boulder, alone. Sitting in church "faking" to be okay, was wearing on me as well. If something didn't change soon, I was going to burst.

I felt spent physically, spiritually, and emotionally. I had to daily anoint myself with oil and to pray against the spirit of depression that was trying so desperately to penetrate my spirit. Somehow I kept pulling on that one ounce of hope that I had deep in my soul. I was not going to take a beating lying down. I still had some fight left within me. I am a child of God and I will behave as such. As long as I had faith, I had opportunity.

Bigger Than Me

As kids, whenever we would leave our house for any reason, my mom would tell us "don't you embarrass me." I felt like that about God. Whenever I would leave my house for any reason I was not to embarrass Him.

Demons cannot stay in the presence of the Holy Spirit. I knew most of what I was going through were tests from God. However, when Satan sees us being tested, he wants to jump in to do everything he can to cause us to fail. Jesus, Jesus, Jesus, was the name that I called upon, to keep he and his minions away.

While living in CT after my dad's passing, I had a dream of him. In the dream I saw him above the clouds. There was one cloud that was opened in the center like a donut. He was leaning over the center looking down at me. I saw my Aunt Martha and my grandparents next to him. They were my "great cloud of witnesses."

Then I heard my dad say to me, *"Hang in there, Rikki. If you could see what I see about your future, it is greater than anything that I could have ever provided for you."* That dream was over 17 years ago. I have hung on to that dream, by faith, for dear life. This gave me hope, because I knew he was now with God and he could see what was ahead. If my earthly father who was now in heaven told me it was even greater, then that was more than enough to get me through the process.

God's plans for my life are bigger than me. No matter how I try I cannot bring about His plans; I can only live through Him. To be frank, it was extremely hard at times to trust in God while things didn't look like what He promised. This is why we are to walk by faith, and not by sight. There were times that I felt like a failure. It's easy to tell someone that's going through a storm, "hang in there, it's going to be all right." It's another thing to live it.

In The Midst Of Your Storm

Through it all, though it seemed impossible at times, I never gave up on God. I always managed to find my way back into His presence, even when things didn't look like they should. When we learn to lean on Him in ALL things, when we shift our focus to Him, things will take a turn and head in the direction that He is leading us.

We learn to lean on Him in all things.

I wish I could tell some of you that there is a time limit for your storm, but unfortunately, only God knows the times. Meteorologists get their predictions wrong at times. Trust the process. God takes us on faith walks to see what is more important to us. Is it our things or Him that are more valuable to us?

When Job went through his storm, he knew it wasn't because of something that he did wrong. He knew he was a righteous man, and he prayed for his children daily, in the event they weren't living right. After he lost all of his children and all of his possessions, the one thing he didn't lose, was his faith in God. Yes, he got upset with God, but God checked him on it. In the end, Job received double for his trouble. God wants to do the same in our lives when we trust Him. God will turn that situation around so you won't even look like what you've been through.

If at this time you are in the midst of a storm and you have done everything you know to do--you pray, you tithe, are consistent in your attendance at your local church, you read your Bible and you sit and listen to God, please know that God has predestined your day of recovery. Let me encourage you to just hold on, He is going to bless you with everything He has ever promised you. God doesn't take us through hard times to leave us there. How would that glorify Him? He takes us through to see how we will react and behave in the storm and to see if we will lose our faith along the way. Let this encourage you as your faith is strengthened. Don't embarrass God, act like His child and get on through your storm. Greater is coming. How badly do you want double for your trouble from the one true God?

He has unlimited blessings for us. His love for us is immeasurable. He loves us so much that He sent His only Son to die for us! God wants to continue to bless us all the days of our lives. He wants the world to see what He's been working on behind the scenes where no one else could see you going through it.

It's Just A Trim

In the tabernacle, the priests had to trim the wicks back to keep the lampstand burning, in order to shine light in the tabernacle. They did this behind the curtain, where the crowd could not see the trimming. We are the wicks that God continues to trim back, when no one else can see the pain and heartache. But, He is doing it so we can come out shining even brighter.

The aches, the pain, it's all part of the re-alignment process. The surgery was a success. The surgeon is out in the waiting area informing your family of the greater that is coming. It's now time for your recovery!

If you want it badly enough, you will take time to fast, regularly. I fast on a regular schedule, so I can get closer to God. I want to hear from Him, to get close to Him in the throne room, to hear what He wants to whisper to me, things that only He knows. There are days we must sacrifice our time from social media, from television and from our smartphones. Put those things down and pick up an actual Bible. Read through it, write notes in it, and keep a journal of your time with God. How badly do you want everything that God has promised you? Have I mentioned that greater is coming?!

God has some secret things that He wants to share with us during those personal moments with Him. He wants to engage in pillow talk with us. Not everyone is privy to such an encounter. Either they are not in a relationship, or they take that relationship for granted. For those that enjoy the relationship, they take the time at the end of the day to share in pillow talk.

> *God has some secret things that He wants to share with us during those personal moments with Him.*

This is the time when they share their moments of the day with their significant other. Moments only they share with one another. No one else gets to listen in on this conversation; this is just between the two in the relationship. Make the time to have pillow talk with God. Give God some of that intimate time and watch Him share those secret things with you. He's worth it and He will see you through your darkest hours. Rest in His arms as you recover.

Recovering

Strengthening Wings

There wasn't a particular day on my calendar that was marked as my actual turning point. I know it was a slow, steady process coming out of the storm that I was in. It took me months to get my finances together. I was in recovery mode. Suddenly I went from being nestled up in a cocoon during my transformation, into a beautiful butterfly. Did you know that when a butterfly exits the cocoon it takes up to four hours before it can fly? The wings are not strong enough coming out of that stage to take off immediately. There is another process of strengthening, to allow the blood to flow through the wings, so it can soar.

As I too began to strengthen my wings, I slowly paid on things that I could handle at the time. I did my best to work with creditors that didn't understand that I didn't have the money to pay them. If I had the money they wanted, then there would be no need for them to contact me. That wasn't reason enough for them, so they continued to call and I continued to work with what was given to me.

During this recovery it was important to me to remain a tither. I wanted to prove to God that I could be trusted with the finances that He provided to me, and I was a good steward over that income. If we manage poorly and put tithing on the "if I could give it after I pay for everything else" list, then He knows He can't trust us with more.

I give because I know that the Giver who is giving back to me, will never run out of blessings. I do it out of obedience to God. Give and it shall be given back to you. God, I need you to overflow my cup! As a matter of fact, I have empty barrels waiting to be filled with your blessings, so I can be a blessing to others. I no longer want to be a receiver of the blessings, I want to be the one who blesses others.

After I started the temporary assignment, I never took on a second job to get ahead financially. That would have taken away my time for photography. I had to sharpen my skills as a photographer, so I could spend time building my photography business. The management team at my apartment complex worked with me when my rent was late. I managed to make payment arrangements with my other utility providers; I was im recovery mode. This was God's favor in action, my wings were getting stronger.

Then one day I was offered a permanent job. Which meant steady income. It wasn't the highest paying job but it was stable and more than I was making as a temp. Now, I was that butterfly that discovered I had wings. Little flutters began to happen when I made this discovery.

Joseph went from the pit, to the prison, then to the palace. I went from the customer service position as a temp, to a permanent position as an administrative coordinator in a better location. Look out palace here I come.

After his dreams, Joseph didn't see the pit or the prison coming. He knew that one day he'd be in a position of authority. He was going to govern a nation. I never imagined the same route, but I do know of the same results. Victory in my divine destiny. The entire purpose has yet to be revealed to me, but I know I am on my way.

L.I.P.

I was no longer stressed about not having enough money to survive; I was now getting caught up on the old debt. My wings are starting to flap. I found that giving my tithes and offerings got me out of my debt a lot faster. I could have held on to that "extra" money by not giving my tithes, but then I would be robbing God. Flap wings, flap.

Photography jobs began to pick up, that was additional income. I could see God's hand in getting me on the other side of my storm. All I could remind myself of was that "this, too, shall pass." I was beginning to recover. My wings are getting stronger. I was living in my present and praying to make it to my destiny. One day at a time. Whenever we are faced with storms in our lives-- car breaks down, no longer employed, bills are due but money is short, just remember, "this, too, shall pass." We serve a God who loves us and is kind; through those storms He protects and defends us. Only God can turn our situations from nothing into something. I learned to abide under the shadow of the almighty. He became my refuge.

It was in 2006 that I did my first professional wedding as a photographer. Slowly I started adding other weddings and high school seniors. Taking on those photography jobs caused me to build a company … wait for it … I am now the founder and CEO of L.I.P. by Rikki, LLC ~ Lasting Impressions Photography. I am walking in my purpose on my way to my divine destiny.

I created a digital vision board and a physical vision wall; there are times when a board just isn't big enough to hold all that you are expecting God to do in your life. I have cut out and taped pictures of things that I know He said I could have. I have maps of the places that I want to travel to, international and domestic trips. A picture of my mansion is on there as well as the details of the lot of land that I will one day possess.

There are times when a board just isn't big enough to hold all that you are expecting God to do in your life.

I am a seed of Abraham, a daughter of the King. I am destined to live a life of royalty. I have scriptures displayed on both boards to read aloud each time I stand before the wall, trusting in God to reward me, double for my trouble.

Looking over my inventory that God instructed me to take in September 2009, of all the things we lost, I can say that I have recovered it all. My place is now fully furnished where I've actually outgrown my apartment. I have a new 2013 Subaru Legacy, and I donated my van to my church, The Worship Center. I am managing my money to the penny, so God can trust me with much more. I am expecting greater to the point where I have FIVE different personal bank accounts. Each account represents the FIVE black trash bags that I had in my possession when I left my "Egypt."

I Am Expecting

When I went into one of the banks to open an account, the manager asked me why I wouldn't only bank with them only. I pondered her question for a moment, and then confidently told her that "one day soon, I was going to be a multimillionaire, and one bank couldn't insure all of my money." To this day when she sees me coming, she reminds me of my millions that are on the way.

I opened these accounts based on some wisdom I gathered in the storm. The bank only insures up to $125,000 of our money. In the present I am making preparations for what I am expecting in my future. That's God's promise to me. I have multiple savings accounts. I have stocks and bonds. I don't have my millions in them at the moment but I am expecting!

A couple expecting a child gets the room ready and the house set for the new addition to the family. People bringing a pet home for the first time make preparations. Why is it not the same thing for the children of God to make preparations for what they are expecting of Him? We need to do the same concerning the promises of God. "Oh ye of little faith" is not my motto. Noah had to make ready for the flood. How that story would be different if he hadn't.

The foundation has been laid for the "and then some" that is coming into my life. I am expecting nothing but the great. I didn't go through this, just to end up with what I had when I started. God has not brought me through such a storm, only to recover what I once had. He has greater in store for me. As I continue on the road to the overage, He continues to give me revelation of the great cause.

A stream of finances is needed in the kingdom. There are people that desire a house of worship. God wants to be represented well. It is an insult to God to have our houses look better than His house of worship. It is my desire to help build up my local church, The Worship Center, in Columbus, Ohio. We look nice now, but we have to make ready for what's to come. We will have the latest technology, and a church for children to come and grow. We need to reach the masses, to introduce the unsaved to Christ. This house of worship will be known for miracles, signs, and wonders. Preparation is in effect.

I realized that having come through the storm successfully, having the foundation for my company, my home and my career laid; this time God's way. It is so solid that nothing can tear it down. With the foundation in place I am ready to build a legacy for my children's children upon it.

Accepting NO Limits

Chapter Six
It's Not Just About You

The Fourth Generation: *Rova*

"Who can count the dust of Jacob, and the number of the fourth part of Israel?"
~ NUMBERS 23:10 NKJV

"A good man leaves an inheritance to his children's children. But the wealth of the sinner is stored up for the righteous."
~ PROVERBS 13:22 NKJV

There were times when the dreams that God gave me were bigger than who I was. That's where my faith came in. It wasn't something I could bring to pass, but I had to wait on God's manifestation. After all that I have gone through, I knew it wasn't just about me. I knew I was pushing through for generations to come.

Here is a partial journal entry from (November 8, 2007):

> *"There is much to be done, but You God can turn my situation around. You can restore back to me. You can make it all possible. Everything You said, I know I will see its manifestation in my life. I walk in my power and authority. I know my rights as Your child. You've given me my faith, You've given me my confidence in You. You've given me liberty. You've given me my desires. I know You did not bring me to this point of my life to leave me like this, with nothing. I know I am not going through these difficult times just for me. It's for me and the generations that follow. They will know the God that I serve, that I trust and believe in. You've taken me to another level of faith but I am excited for the opportunity to be a witness and a testimony for you!"*

From the time God delivered the children of Israel out of bondage in Egypt, to today, He still uses people to be a blessing to His kingdom. People who are humble enough to give God the glory when success happens, are the ones He uses to participate in His purpose.

> *"Then he (Pharaoh) called for Moses and Aaron by night, and said, 'Rise and go out from among my people, both you and the children of Israel. And go, serve the Lord as you have said. Also, take your flocks and your herds as you have said, and be gone; and bless me also.' And the Egyptians urged the people, that they might send*

> *them out of the land in haste. For they said, 'We shall all be dead.' So the people took their dough before it was leavened, having their kneading bowls bound up in their clothes on their shoulders. Now the children of Israel had done according to the word of Moses, and they had asked from the Egyptians articles of silver, articles of gold, and clothing. And the Lord had given the people favor in the sight of the Egyptians, so that they granted them what they requested. Thus they plundered the Egyptians."*
> ~ EXODUS 12:31-36 NKJV

When God sends us out to do His will, He will send us with everything that we need. As He blesses us, even with our enemy's possessions, it's not just for our own personal gain. He has a plan and a purpose for blessing His people.

This is why we go through stages of testing. If we pass the tests, He knows He can trust us, with the assignment to do His will. If we fail, He moves on. One truth I discovered about God is that He doesn't need us we need Him.

For His Purpose

When He delivered the children with their enemy's plunder, it was for the purpose of His kingdom in their lives, as they journeyed on to the Promise Land to worship and serve their God.

> *"And Moses spoke to all the congregation of the children of Israel, saying. 'This is the thing which the Lord commanded, saying: 'Take from among you an offering to the Lord. Whoever is of a willing heart, let him bring it as an offering to the Lord; gold, silver, and bronze; blue and purple and scarlet yarn, fine linen thread,*

> *and goats' hair; rams' skins dyed red, badger skins, and acacia wood; oil for the light, and spices for the anointing oil and for the sweet incense; onyx stones, and stones to be set in the ephod and in the breastplate."*
> *- EXODUS 35:4-9 NKJV*

Think about it, they weren't warriors so they couldn't go into a preoccupied land and take what they needed, without being defeated. They lacked confidence, but they had to fulfill their purpose. God prepared them before entering in with what they would need to fulfill His assignment. God gave them a "loan" they would never have to pay back.

God provided the children of Israel with the resources that were required for the building of the Tabernacle. What they plundered from their enemy, they used for the House of God! They didn't have to work years after being enslaved for the materials required for the House of God. God delivered them out of bondage with the very things they were going to need, in the wilderness. Those who had a WILLING heart, were the ones that gave of their possessions.

God will never deliver us without provision in our delivered state. In fact, He will provide in abundance. When we start to give from a willing heart for the building of His kingdom out of the abundance that He has provided unto us, He will tell us "STOP! That's too much."

> *God will never deliver us without provision in our delivered state.*

Wouldn't you like to be in a position of abundance of provision that you want to bless the church you are attending for the up building of the kingdom, only to hear them say, *"STOP! That's too much?"* (Exodus 36:6-7 NKJV), *"So Moses gave a commandment, and they caused it to be proclaimed throughout the camp, saying, 'Let neither man nor woman do any more work for the offering of the sanctuary. And the people were restrained from bringing, for the material they had was sufficient for all the work to be done—indeed too much.'"* That's Bible.

My response to that is; Lord, use me. What I been through and what God delivered me out of, God made provisions for me. Lord, in my life continue to give so I can give to Your work. It's not just for me; it's for the generations to come. The wealth that I am building, it's not just for me; it's for the generations to come. What has been sealed in heaven will be revealed on earth.

My prayer has always been for God to make my life here on earth reflect heaven. Streets of gold, gates of pearls, peace, joy, dancing, praise, rejoicing and a life of peace on earth as it is in heaven, this side of heaven. That's how I see myself in this lifetime.

To get to this place of believing God for the impossible, it requires prayer and time with God to strengthen your faith. Wandering around in the wilderness before entering into my Promised Land, made me feel at times that God abandoned me. I was hearing the doubters, hearing the hacklers, and those that were envious, caused doubt to enter in, even for a moment.

If we allow this "noise" to enter in, then it further separates us from the one resource that can get through. Being with God allowed time for me to renew my hope, and strengthen my spirit man to journey on. Never losing my focus on the One who called me into His game plan, got me through the cocoon stage that transformed me.

Here is another journal entry:

Psalm 32:8 NKJV

> *"I will instruct you and teach you in the way you should go; I will guide you with My eye."*

This was the scripture given to me by the Holy Spirit that day. "While I was in Your presence this morning it was revealed to me that all along You've been looking for a friend that You can trust with the things that You have, but also with what You want to do. You want to be sure that they won't steal Your 'thunder.' The things that You have promised me are byproducts of my relationship and fellowship with You. No, You are not 'buying' me, I have been tested, I have been tried. I have passed because I know that I want my relationship with You above everything else. All those around me will benefit because of that ... to be used by You for Your will."

As we see throughout the entire Old Testament, God is about family. Since the flood; He saved an entire family to start a new population of a potentially obedient generation. The children of Israel had the mandate to pass down their stories from generation to generation so that everything that God had done for them it wouldn't be lost on their families.

I have done my best to document and share my Christian experience since the beginning of my relationship with God. It's so important for the generations coming after us to know about the God that we serve. The God that can make ways out of no way. The God that makes impossible things happen. The God that takes the ordinary and makes it extraordinary. The God that takes natural and makes it supernatural. Who wouldn't want to serve a God like Him? God wants to bless His children with the best of everything. People need to see something divine, something not of this world. They need to see God.

What He Inspires, He Will Provide

I remember a dream where He showed me an estate. I will never forget what I saw in the dream. Some of it I wrote down, (though those papers that were in the storage that I no longer have) and trusting that when the time comes to own it, He will bring it back to my remembrance.

Here in New Albany, I always felt that this was the place where I would purchase my first home. Never in all of my 51 years on this earth have I owned a home.

The house He showed me, in my Promised Land, will be well worth the wait. There were many highs and lows, excitement and disappointment, along the way. There were many days that I thought, "this is the day of the manifestation," only to end the day in disappointment. Along the way, He has shown me where, He has told me which realtor to work with, and He even allowed me to meet the builder one day while I was out looking at a home that he was overseeing the construction process for. All of this was my preparation. We want God to hasten the process, but some things just can't be rushed.

It wasn't until He revealed to me the layout of the house, inside and out, that I knew this was bigger than me. Here is a dream that I had and journaled on April 30, 2008:

> *I was a spectator as the Holy Spirit was guiding me around a celebration. It looked like a scene from a movie, something like out of Africa. There was a wealthy couple attending a wedding and I was watching part of the reception. The woman was very sad as she looked on! She had no children of her own and she was sitting, watching and clapping to the music as others danced. Her husband was standing behind her with a hand perched upon her shoulder. They both understood that there was no immediate family to inherit their fortune. Then the men came and each grabbed an end of the rods, elevated her and carried her away. They were her "chariot." She and her husband were dressed in the finest of clothes.*
>
> *The interpretation: When I awoke I had no clue! Since I wasn't in it, but observed, I had no idea. I walked the dogs and that's when You gave me the interpretation. You said "transference of wealth." That is what happens and how it happens. When what belongs to the wealthy,*

it is all Yours, they may not have anyone to leave it to but You do! Transference of wealth!!!

Just as God gave the children of Israel their enemy's plunder as they were being delivered from their hands, is the same way He will provide a transference of wealth for me to have more than enough for the up building of His kingdom, and to leave an inheritance for my children's children, *"A good man leaves an inheritance to his children's children. But the wealth of the sinner is stored up for the righteous"* (Proverbs 13:22 NKJV).

I don't know how God will do all that He said He is going to do in my life but my part isn't to figure that out, my part is to have faith to know that it's going to happen, this side of heaven. That God will fund this greater purpose that is larger than my imagination.

Too many times He has reminded me that it's all for His glory. It is for me to receive and give all the glory to God for all that He has done and will do. God didn't make me to be ordinary. I saw that as a child and having those dreams.

When He created me, He imparted class and sophistication into my life. I am created for royalty. I am in the family of the King, so I expect royalty in my life. I am representing my Daddy, the King. Ever since I can remember, the quality of life was always one that only some people dream of that can be unattainable. God has given me dreams, hope, and promises of the best of the best.

> *God will cause us to have desires for the things in which He created us for.*

God will cause us to have desires for the things in which He created us for. Those desires and passions draw us to our purpose. Our purpose has a magnetic design to pull us in that direction.

What is your desire? What is your passion? What you are passionate about will get you out of bed on days you don't feel like it. It will energize you all day long. Find that passion, and walk in your purpose. Don't allow people to limit you in how God has designed you. Let the haters hate, because the only one you need to please is God.

In order for me to get the house and the other things He promised, it will require money; hence, the transference of wealth. I am not worried about losing it all EVER again. My success of having passed that test, will keep me from repeating the process. I have gained wisdom and knowledge to treat money with respect, to know where every dollar will go, I am expecting overflow.

Know where your dollars and cents are at all times. Don't just ball up the money and throw the change around in your pocket or purse. Don't just leave it lying around the house. Respect the things God has given to you and watch Him bless you with so much more.

Here is another journal entry regarding the estate: May 6, 2008 at 7:28 a.m.

> *"On yesterday I felt directed to have a realtor look for 5 – 10 acres of land in New Albany, OH so I can have a house built. It will have a six car heated garage, a unit to wash the cars. It will have an in-law suite, a swimming pool, tennis court and basketball court. At least 10 bedrooms! "*

For a quick moment the enemy tried to rob me of that dream that God gave to me. Questioning why I would need something so elaborate? I then was reminded of David and Solomon. The "house" that Solomon built for God was worth $586 BILLION dollars! This house was for God. David had a palace, as did Solomon. Those were the things that God gave to them. I will take the house that God has purposed for me. I will gladly take the elaborate.

There is no such thing as God's children having too much. I want God to spoil me; I'll take all of it and share it with those He tells me to bless. It's about His kingdom business and purpose, and I just happened to be one of His children who is being used by Him to fulfill that purpose. Use me up Lord, have Your way in my life.

If God has given you a dream or a vision and it seems bigger than you, it may scare you but don't be afraid of it. Embrace it and don't allow the enemy to take it away from you. It's up to us to protect what God has given to us. The devil knows if we are broke and disgusted we cannot make an impact in God's kingdom. It cost money to finance a church.

Big Ideas

God wants to find people He can trust with His finances to move His kingdom forward and not to spend only on themselves. Can He trust you? Do we give of our tithes and offerings? Do we give to special programs or donate to other organizations like human trafficking or the homeless shelters to further assist others? It's not just about you; it's about sharing our testimony so others can come to Christ.

God has shared with me two major business ideas, in addition to the photography. They all tie together and will go hand in hand. I received one of the two in December of 2016.

One idea is to start a safe house for people that want out of the human trafficking ring here in Ohio, and then eventually it will expand across the globe. One night while I was reading through *Chase the Lion* by Mark Batterson, he stated, "If your dream doesn't scare you, it's too small." My prayer was, "God, what more do you want me to do with my photography? What more am I to do to qualify my dream as big?"

I wasn't surprised to find my answer in a dream. That night He shared with me how I am to start the safe house for people that have cried out to Him that want out, but have no place to go. Not everyone wants to be in that trafficking ring, and those that want out He has heard their cry.

I have to say, after I awoke and remembered, the dream I was a little shaken by the thought of getting involved with this aspect of society. Wait. What. Me? Immediately I heard, "It's not like I'm asking you to take on the Cartel." You can only imagine that if I weren't already lying down, I would have fell all the way out after that remark. God has such an amazing sense of humor.

I have ideas in place for this safe house. I've since attended a conference regarding human trafficking here in Columbus, Ohio. The statistics alone broke my heart. I have meetings in place with a few people to staff this house, as I have no experience in this regard, but I have a Business Partner that will lead the charge.

The other idea that was shared with me was back in 2001. It is a business idea called R.O.P.E. 4 Life (Recipient of Program Excellence). This program will allow people to go through nine-months of training (hmmm, wonder where that idea came from) to get them ready for the workforce. Upon completion of the program, they will go through three weeks of preparation, for on-the-job interviews. This will include building a resume, how to dress for success, grooming, personal financing and setting up bank accounts.

Once they have secured a job and have kept it for three months, they will be connected to Habitat for Humanity, where they will be able to secure an opportunity to work on building their very own home, with a mortgage they can afford.

With R.O.P.E. 4 Life and the Daughters of Deborah safe house my dream is pretty big. It scares me in a good way because it's so big that I know I can't do this without God.

Another favorite book of mine is *Praying for Your Elephant* by Adam Stadtmiller. Praying for your "elephant" is to pray for something that is so large, that it requires God's involvement. "The boundaries of our personal prayer lives often have less to do with biblical restrictions, and more to do with the limitations we place on them." I now have my elephant sized prayers for God to do exceedingly, abundantly, more than I can ask or think.

I can see and now fully understand the need of a wealth transfer. I have worked years with Habitat for Humanity. I have gone through a business school, and only took nine-months to complete it. I am in a prime location to help those wanting out of a life of trafficking to make something better for themselves. Don't ever count your experiences as a waste. This is all part of God's preparation for our purpose.

Don't allow the devil to steal your praise when you are going through those experiences. If he steals that from us then He's stealing that away from God. God wants to inhabit the praises of His people. When we succeed that means God succeeds.

In *Hebrew Word Study* Chaim Bentorah wrote the following:

> *"Four 'Generations' in Our Relationship with God. I remember watching a presentation on the television program NOVA about the monarch butterfly. Every year, the fourth generation of the monarch butterfly will take a three-month journey. These butterflies will travel fifty miles a day from all parts of Canada, converge in Texas, and then fly down to one spot on a mountain in Mexico, arriving at almost the same time. Millions of them all arrive on this one mountain. What caught my attention was that it is the fourth generation that makes this thirty-five-hundred-mile trip. The documentary explained how many of the butterflies suffer and die while making this journey. They perish from the elements or from predators. In fact, as I write this*

study, this year's monarch butterflies are currently on that journey to their 'promised land,' and they should be passing over my home in the Chicago area about now.

"Is the monarch butterflies yearly journey a sign, or reminder, from God? If so, what is the nature of this reminder? The sages teach that not only is there something special about each fourth generation, but there are also four 'generations' in our relationship with God. The first is our spiritual birth—I consider this to be our rebirth in Jesus Christ. The second is our growth period. The third is our wilderness period. The fourth is our entrance into the Promised Land. If you feel like you've been wandering in the wilderness, as the Israelites were at the time of Balaam, and if you feel like you are getting nowhere and accomplishing nothing, as Israel must have felt, then you need to look up and see the monarch butterflies flying to Mexico, because they are a reminder that you are approaching that fourth generation, and the Promised Land is in sight. You may have to face a few more storms and a few more predators, but if you can continue your journey, you will arrive on the mountaintop where, like the monarchs, you can rest from your long journey."

I didn't go looking for those promises, daily I ask the Holy Spirit to lead me and I'll follow as He leads. Some days are just to pray. Other days are to fast. However He leads me I will follow.

> *Daily I ask the Holy Spirit to lead me and I'll follow as He leads.*

Spy Out The Land

Today (August 15, 2016) was another day that He led me to a realtors website and I happened upon a posting for a property of 5 – 10 acres, and it just so happened that my mom and daughter were in town during this time. I finally had the chance to publicly share these dreams with them.

I was led to contact a loan officer at one of my banks for the property, and contract loan, just to gather information to continue making preparations for what I am expecting God to do. After making contact with him and getting the financial information, we were off to spy out the land.

> *"And the Lord spoke to Moses, saying, send men to spy out the land of Canaan, which I am giving to the children of Israel. So Moses sent them to spy out the land of Canaan, and said to them, 'go up this way into the South, and go up to the mountains, and see what the land is like; whether the people who dwell in it are strong or weak, few or many; whether the land they dwell in is good or bad; whether the cities they inhabit are like camps or strongholds; where the land is rich or poor; and whether there are forests there or not. Be of good courage. And bring some of the fruit of the land."*
> ~ NUMBERS 14:1-2, 17-20 NKJV

I truly believe that my mom and daughter caught the vision that God has shared with me years ago. My daughter saw what I had been hearing all these years. I think she could see that I was believing God for these promises to happen, so the generations to come will know that the one true living God still moves mountains and blesses His children. We've come a long way from sleeping in the car that one night in Syracuse, NY, to surveying 5-10 acres of land to build our house on.

I never had that opportunity to go to college to become that architect but I will still have the opportunity to design my own house! These are the desires that God places within us for our purpose. I may not have that college degree, and that's okay with me as I have my Ph.D in tote.

That is how I will be able to help others, with my experiences in the prophetic, healing, and deliverance.

There are times when we will have to step out on faith and "spy out" the land and bring a good report back to God. If we doubt, it will keep us out of the land longer than it should take.

I now have more information today about purchasing land than I did the day before. I walked out on the property and did a drive through, to "see" how I want things laid out in the Promised Land. I saw the vision that God has for me, and now I walked the land to see what God saw. I may not have anything tangible at this time, but I do have faith.

The "fruit" of the land are photos that I have of the land. This house isn't just for me. He has plans to bring it all together. In 2006, when He told me to do just photography, I now see that it's to document where I am going, and the success of the people who will be going through the program. I will be able to do photo sessions with them, something they may not have been able to afford otherwise.

I will host various fundraisers and, it will allow me to host different parties / dinners at the house. I can have holiday parties for those that live here in Ohio, and don't have family here to celebrate with them. There are many reasons that He has shown me how to use this house. But know this one thing about me; if it were just for me to enjoy it because He wants to "spoil" me, I would be fine with that as well. Who wouldn't want their daddy to spoil them? It's my time to be spoiled.

Accepting NO Limits

Chapter SEVEN
Ready to Soar

Breath: *Neshimah*

"Let everything that has breath praise the Lord."
~ PSALM 150:6 NKJV

"But those who wait on the Lord shall renew their strength; they shall mount up with wings like eagles. They shall run and not be weary, they shall walk and not faint."
~ ISAIAH 40:31 NKJV

I know that my story will not end without receiving everything that God has designed for me and for that I will praise the Lord. In everything that I do, in everything that I endured, for the rest of my life, everyday that I breathe, I will praise the Lord. He has done amazing things in my life. He has brought me through the good and the bad. Even in my worst choices, He has never left me. I am not perfect but I am faithful. If I were to die today, without seeing another promise come to pass, I will be in glory praising the Lord forevermore.

God's desire for us is to be a beacon of light in dark places. *"Let your light so shine before men, that they may see your good works and glorify your Father in heaven"* (Matthew 5:16 NKJV). The culture where God has placed me needs to see my light. God has brought me through my darkest days successfully, and is using my story to draw others to Him.

My dreams and visions will come to pass. I continue to push through to opportunities that God has provided for me, accepting no limits, as I enter into my divine destiny. There is a world hungry to see something divine, something that's not of this world.

If you are dealing with some dark days in your life, find a way to praise the Lord. Get away from the crowd of people and the noise all around you; take time to enter into His presence. One of my favorite scriptures is in Isaiah 55 where even the trees clap their "hands," *"For you shall go out with joy, and be led out with peace; the mountains and the hills shall break forth into singing before you, and all the trees of the field shall clap their hands. Instead of the thorn shall come up the cypress tree, and instead of the brier shall come up the myrtle tree; and it shall be to the Lord for a name, for an everlasting sign that shall not be cut off."*

If God can cause nature to praise Him, then why do we hold back our praise when we are going through? Praise your way out. Praise Him in advance for your expectancy. Confuse the enemy and praise God in spite of your circumstances. Praise will lighten your burdens. I will not have any rock crying out for me. Have you ever really looked at a rock? It's dead weight, why would I let something that doesn't have breath praise in my place?

If this was you, and you allowed rocks to cry out and trees to clap their hands in your place, ask God right now for forgiveness in your selfishness and give Him some praise. Our praise shall be a sign to the Lord of our gratitude and love and thanking Him for our prosperity and good health. That's the kind of God that people want to serve. If you are grateful, put this book down (only for a moment) and give God some undignified praise. Go on, give Him some praise.

Well, now didn't that feel refreshing?

Never Let His Promises Go

So many times I could have given up. I had a legitimate reason not to see this through. But I had an even better reason to stay in it. Through and through, these trials have brought me closer to God; I am on another level of trust. My faith has increased in ways I could not have imagined. I am not the same person or in the same place than I was even two years ago.

I have confidence in God to see me through to my best days yet. God wouldn't build me up to let me fall. What purpose would it serve God to show me the things that He's going to do and not do them? His purpose is to show the world that He is still God and He wants others to serve Him. If you don't get anything else from this book, just know that what God has said, it WILL come to pass. It will not return unto Him void. It will accomplish what it was sent forth to do.

Don't allow anyone to talk you out of your blessings, not even yourself. The only thing you should hear yourself doing during your transformation, is praising Him. It's your promise from God; it's your fight to protect what He has given to you. Are you going to fight or are you going to be defeated? I choose this day to fight in the spirit for my destiny. I will praise my way through.

Defend what is yours. Cover it in prayer. There is a nation of people waiting on you to finish the race. Your success and your light, will allow God to draw them to Himself. Come on beautiful butterfly. It's your time now; your wings have gotten stronger. It's time to take flight.

> *Defend what is yours. Cover it in prayer.*

You may be the next great chef. You may be the next hall of famer. You may be the next Golden Globe winner. You may be the next multi-millionaire. Fly butterfly, fly. But if you give up, if you give in, your next will be someone else's opportunity for God to use. Then that person will become the next butterfly to take flight. Daily I remind myself that God doesn't need me, I need God.

Every day I get to live above ground, is another day that is a gift from God, another opportunity for me to lift up praise with every breath I breathe. I am ever so grateful to God, that He has kept His hand on me and allowed no harm to come near my home or my daughter during this time. Every time I think of the goodness of God, my soul gets excited and I want to run in praise. God is faithful to His word; He is faithful to His children even when we are faithless.

When we fully grasp the understanding of God's love toward us, the confidence that builds within will cause us to endure, to get through the battles, to face our mountains head on knowing that we will inherit the land, to rest and enjoy it for the remainder of our lives. We won't always be in battle, our days of rest are coming.

In *Hebrew Word Study* Chaim Bentorah wrote:

> *"… Before you go to sleep at night or enter into any activity that will distract you from the presence of God, command your soul to bless and praise the Lord. Then, every breath you take will be in praise to God, and you may discover what Paul meant when he said, "Pray without ceasing." Everything you do and say will be as unto God. You will find that once you enter God's heart, you can remain there even while working at your job, cleaning the house, taking an exam, or doing any other activity where you would not normally think about Him. If you command your soul to praise the Lord during that activity, your soul will praise Him even when you are not consciously thinking about Him. May every breath, or neshimah, that you take today be in praise to God."*

In time, God will strengthen you as you feel yourself getting weary in the "valley." I want to strongly encourage you not to get ahead of God, but to wait on Him. Cause your soul to praise Him in that valley. In Psalm 103:1 David caused his breath to praise the Lord, he commanded it to bless the Lord. We have to become more sensitive to the presence of God.

Most times we don't even realize how He's always around us. Every time we "vent" or "complain" in His name, He's there, responding, "Yes, you called on Me?" Only to realize in our frustration we were using His name in vain.

God wants us to stop being so busy using our breath on things that will not change our situation. Let's use our breath in praise, and watch our situation change for the better. Appreciate the breath that He is giving us this side of heaven, to offer up a praise, of gratitude and not an attitude.

He cares for you and He will see you through. We have the right not to accept the lies. Don't allow the enemy to discourage you or to cause you to doubt when the floods come rushing in. Prayer and anointing oil are your life jackets, put them on and swim to the other side of your storm. God will get the glory from our success. He wants us to be successful for this very reason.

When we grow weary, God will cause us to "mount up with wings as eagles." A female bald eagle's body length varies from 35 to 37 inches; with a wingspan of 79 to 90 inches. The smaller male bald eagle has a body length of 30 to 34 inches; with a wingspan ranging from 72 to 85 inches. That means that their wings are much large than their body. When we are feeling weighted down by life, when our bodies grow weary in well doing, God is mounting us up with wings as eagles to carry us through those difficult times.

Take a fighter's stance, plant your stronger foot in the rear, arms extended to the left and right, expand your wings, get ready to soar above your situations.

It's time to take flight. It's time to soar over the problems instead of walking through them. God will elevate us and just like the eagle, we will have sharper, perfect vision. Things will become clearer because we are now above our circumstances. We will glide into our destiny no matter what is going on beneath us.

Get ready to soar because God is like a mother eagle. He knows we've been strengthened while in the cocoon in prayer and reading His word. He knows we are strong enough to soar. So He pushes us out of the nest, our place of comfort, to enter in to our destiny. Fly eagle, fly.

You are now strong enough to receive how you've been seeing yourself in your future. You no longer have to peep into your future. It's now time to live a prosperous life and to be in good health. It's now time for you to move into that five-bedroom home, with that massive king size bed that's now yours. It's time to stand in a homeless shelter feeding those less fortunate, a shelter that you built and are now providing for others. God wants you to see yourself, as He sees you, fearfully and wonderfully made. You were created for such a time as this. A time when people no longer believe or think about miracles. They have lived in such a dry place, that they don't get excited about serving God anymore. They need to see something divine. That something is God working it out through you.

As God led me along the way, I documented and kept a journal so I wouldn't forget the things that He shared with me. As He directed me in the ways to go, in becoming a travel photographer, I could see the pieces starting to fall into place.

Miracles Unfolding

Earlier in the book I shared my desire to travel. Again, how God will give us the desires to fulfill our purpose. I wanted to see what was outside of Connecticut. It became a mission of mine to see all 50 States and other countries.

During this time of recovery it seemed impossible. Then my life began to take a turn. I started to see things turning in my favor. Alyssa graduated from Syracuse University with her Bachelor's and from Florida International University with her Master's. I could not have been any more proud of her accomplishments, or so I thought. She received employment immediately following her graduation from FIU. It's an incredible blessing to have a mature, employed, educated adult child. God is true to His word.

After that push out of the nest right into my purpose, I began to soar. I no longer had to wait on my tax refunds to catch up on my rent and my utilities. Blessings began to trickle in and add up. I was getting used to the purpose of having wings to soar. I began to travel again, even if it were long weekends. The bigger picture had come into focus. I only dreamt of going to other countries, and saw myself traveling as I read the books written by Danielle Steel. And now I was no longer just reading about other characters in her books, it was finally going to be happening for me, a girl from Connecticut.

Why Not Iceland?

In September of 2015, Alyssa and I were given the opportunity to take our first International trip. I now had a passport, and was ready to get it stamped. Going from no money to pay for gas and rent, to purchasing a passport was a miracle in my eyes. Those days when I peeped into my future, I saw myself traveling, so I made preparations for my expectations.

Alyssa and I traveled to Iceland as our first International trip; our first trip across the "pond." This part of my life started to look and feel like what God told me would happen. The long nights, the tears, the disappointments, were now in my past. My future became brighter. This was no longer just a dream, I began living the dream. My soaring had just begun. His promises started to manifest in my life. This contributed to the strengthening of my faith. I had faith to get me through and now I have stronger faith to continue the course.

Iceland is such an incredible place to visit. I was in another country capturing beauty through the eyes of God just as He said I would. We learned so much about another culture--how they live, what they eat and wear. One of the things we noticed was that the people in Iceland are so happy there. Because I am curious by nature, one day we stopped in the lobby of the hotel to ask why this was the case. The concierge kindly told us, "It's in the water." Icelandic water is natural spring water that runs through the lava rocks and is purified. I had to get a hold of this spring water that he so graciously informed us of. I am a witness that after one sip of that Icelandic water I am now a "water snob." The water is noticeably smooth and clean. It was a must have everywhere we went during that trip.

Since this was our first International trip to a country where no one we knew had ever been, we merely booked the trip with no plans in place during our stay that week.

Upon our arrival from what we seen of the country, from the plane, to our hotel, I knew we had to get out and see more of it with people that knew about it. We stopped in the hotel lobby to put tours together during our stay.

One of the tours included the "must see" Blue Lagoon while in Iceland. We boarded the commuter bus and came upon this lava field. Right in the center of this field was this breathtaking geothermal spa out in the open. Though it may be freezing outside during their winter seasons, this didn't stop people from going in. The temperature of this lagoon water averages 99-102 *F. Many documentaries, television shows and movies have been filmed at this lagoon and now we've been blessed to not only see it, but to be in it. God is faithful.

On another tour we went to the waterfalls to see the spring water in action. This tour took us to see the glaciers. Location after location, volcanoes and mountains, walking through the national parks, all gave me photo opportunities that seemed never ending. I was walking in my purpose.

Of course we needed to eat and we discovered how amazingly tasteful the Mediterranean food really is. The island is a place that I tell everyone that asks, "Why Iceland?" and my response is, "Why not Iceland?" Iceland is so beautiful, that it is on my "revisit" list. We stopped to visit a museum to find out the history of Iceland. We even enjoyed a day of horseback riding to get another perspective of the island. This island truly is a well-hidden gem.

Just as God had said, I was now in my element as a travel photographer. This trip has earned me the title of an International Travel Photographer, how's that for overflow? God did that thing! Right there on the island of Iceland, with my daughter along with me, God's promises began to manifest for us.

"Capturing beauty through the eyes of God," is my company slogan; my "mission statement" if you will. Photos from this trip will make it into my photo gallery one day. I have not forgotten that promise from God; to have my work displayed for the world to see. It's all part of letting my light shine before men, so He can draw people to Himself. To God be the glory!

> *I have not forgotten that promise from God, to have my work displayed for the world to see.*

Upon our return to the States, one day I was in my local grocery store, in the water aisle, and as I looked up I saw a bottle labeled "Icelandic Glacial!" Could it be? Icelandic spring water was in MY grocery store? It was, and I bought every bottle on the shelves. It's not such a popular item in Ohio at the moment, but as long as this one grocery store keeps it stocked I will be a happy individual, after all, "it's in the water." Yes, I am a full fledge "water snob," I admit it, and own it.

One of the greatest moments of that trip was being able to go through Customs and getting my passport stamped alongside my daughter. What a difference from sleeping in the car that night in Syracuse, NY, to coming off an International flight! In so many ways, I was soaring to new heights.

I was ready to go places that God said I would be able to go, to do the things that I couldn't afford to do without the finances. God promised me that money will never be an issue for me. My journey is far from over, I haven't received my double portion at this point but I have learned to live in the present. I can capture the moments on "film" and display them for the world to see what God is doing in my life.

There is nothing we cannot do as long as we trust God. All that matters is for His children to feel confident in Him to do just as He said He would do. We hold ourselves back from the God life when we don't trust in Him, when we don't live in His perfect will. As we let go and fall into His arms, He is there to catch us and to shower His favor on us. Seek Him daily. Capture His heart and there is nothing stopping your success.

Only the Beginning

Since our trip to Iceland in 2015, we were afforded another international trip and we have two domestic trips later in 2016. I now have two wall maps displayed in my apartment. One is the map of the United States and the other is The World map. I have pins in the places where I have visited over the years; the unpinned locations remind me of places I have yet to visit. I am keeping the vision before me.

Throughout my apartment, I have many souvenirs of the places where I visited. Some are from here in the States, and now internationally. I started a collection of flags on my wall of the countries I have traveled to. I am still dreaming big, because that's just the kind of God that I serve. The world may tell me no, and there have been many closed doors along the way, but I am accepting no limits.

The second International trip happened in May 2016. This girl right here went to Spain!!!! My daughter that I dragged through my faith walk back in 2007 – 2011 was right there with me. I was over the moon at this point. Pressing through my darkest days were now paying off.

This time we traveled with a group of Syracuse Alums. They put this trip together through a travel agency and they did all of the work for us. The "free" days I used my AAA services to put our tours together for us prior to our departure, a lesson I learned through experience.

From not having enough money for gas, food, and rent and having to take cold showers because I couldn't pay the bill that month, to now having been in Spain! Soar eagle, soar.

We flew into Madrid and stayed for three days. The first night I laid my head down to sleep on a hotel pillow in Spain, I drifted off to sleep with thanksgiving in my heart. While in Madrid we toured the wine country and did bar hops. We were introduced to tapas (appetizers) and found after a few servings of the different tapas, we were full. Madrid is the "party" city we discovered. Another opportunity for more and more photos. We met more amazing people and found high-end shopping areas to purchase items from Spain. The food is as authentic as the country. The wine is out of this world. To God be the glory.

After a few days there, we then took the bullet train to Barcelona. The ride on this train was something I only read about in Danielle Steel's books and saw in movies. This time it was my personal experience. The doors between the cars slid open like something out of a James Bond movie. I was on cloud nine once again. This was now my life.

We spent the rest of our days in Barcelona. At the time of this trip, it was soccer season and Barcelona happened to be playing one night. The city became a ghost town as families gathered around their televisions in their apartments around the city. The bars had crowds of people surrounding the televisions of proud Spaniards cheering on their team. We were in the heart of it all. Surrounded by God's love, I felt like I could feel Him smiling down on us. These are the things dreams are made of, no actress or character in a book. No, this was my life.

Barcelona is the city of art and history. We were privileged to go on three different tours of this amazing city. The sights, the sounds and the people made for more memorable moments captured on camera of course. A few times we dined with three couples and two friends that were traveling together and we became "meal buddies" while in Spain.

As we toured Spain those eight days I couldn't get enough of this magnificent country. There is one place that I tell everyone they must see and that is the Sagrada Familia, it is Antoni Gaudi's life's work. There aren't many places that take my breath away. I recall when Alyssa and I visited the Grand Canyon when she was 10 years old; we reached the outer ring of the Canyon, tears slowly streamed down my face seeing God's handy work firsthand.

When I walked into the Sagrada Familia it was the same reaction, tears slowly streaming down my face. Gaudi designed this cathedral after the life of Christ, from birth to His resurrection. Words don't do this famous landmark justice. This is a must see to understand the phenomena. So thankful for the beauty that I was able to capture on this trip.

As I sat outside on the balcony of a restaurant having dinner overlooking Barcelona, I couldn't help but to think about how awesome God is. My journey has taken a turn into God's perfect will. I am well on my way to my divine destiny. I know that greater is coming as I continue to soar. I am grateful to have taken this journey with my daughter to make lasting memories along the way. Sometimes we lose the "ooh" because we don't live in the moment. We are so focused on what is yet to come and we

I know that greater is coming as I continue to soar.

miss the ooh moments. As I continue this journey, I keep the vision before me without forgetting to live in my present.

This wonderful trip to Spain unfortunately had to come to an end, at least for now. Leaving was bitter sweet. While we were sad to leave, we were ready to head home. We arrived to the airport with time to spare so people sat around in groups that became acquainted with one another on this trip. We exchanged numbers and emails and promised to keep in touch.

We sat around and chatted a bit and "Rick" engaged Alyssa and I in conversation. He was asking her more detailed questions about her education and career. Then we started discussing what I did and about my book, as this trip to Spain came after I committed to writing this book.

He asked about the book, and if I could share some of what I was going to write about. I gave him the "elevator" version and told him that he should be sure to purchase the book, once it's in print, and he said that he couldn't wait to read it. He sat there intently on the edge of his seat listening to my story and asking questions along the way. This was the first time I confessed to Alyssa about not having enough money for the hotel in Syracruse, NY, which caused us to sleep in the car that night. He would nod and shake his head as I continued sharing. Seeing and hearing the reaction of people as I share my book with them and they show great interest is a testament to all that I have been through for God's glory!

As I was nearing the end, he sat straight up in his chair and he said, "I have to ask, how does the story end? Do you recover any of it? Did you get it all back?" Before I could form a response Alyssa replied with a heartfelt, "We're in Spain aren't we?"

~ THE JOURNEY CONTINUES ~

Let's Connect

Rikki Webber

A single mom with a passion for capturing what God sees through His eyes, Rikki L. Webber is an international photographer and the owner of Lasting Impressions Photography. She is an ordained minister of the Gospel and enjoys helping others see their life through the eyes of God, accept no limits, and soar above all circumstances!

To Learn more or to invite Rikki Webber to speak
www.rikkilwebber.com

Accepting NO Limits

Travel Photo Gallery

The Early Years

My House While in High School

Mall in Barcelona, Spain

Sagrada Familia: Roman Catholic Church in Barcelona, Spain

Sagrada Familia: Roman Catholic Church in Barcelona, Spain

Depiction of Christ outside Sagrada Familia in Barcelona, Spain

Statue of Christopher Columbus in Barcelona, Spain

Village in Barcelona, Spain

Center Square in Barcelona, Spain

Center Square in Barcelona, Spain (Another View)

Home of Pablo Picasso (Under Renovation)

Art District in
Barcelona, Spain

Test of Time in Barcelona, Spain

Wisdom in Barcelona, Spain

Alyssa in Barcelona, Spain

The Cellar, Bodegas Jesus Diaz Winery in Madrid, Spain

**Aging to Perfection
Madrid, Spain**

Wine Tour, J.H. Solera Winery: Madrid, Spain

Wine Tour in Madrid, Spain

Winery in Madrid, Spain

Back in Time in Madrid, Spain

By Train
Barcelona, Spain

My James Bond Moment
AVE High Speed Train
Barcelona, Spain

Seeing the World One State at a Time

Where I Began my Relationship with Jesus in Hartford, Connecticut

From Their View in Newport, Rhode Island

Changing of the Guards in Washington, DC

Promises Unfolding (God's Doing It!) in New York, New York

Guiding Light in Portland, Maine

A Light on a Hill in Portland, Maine

Let it Snow: Philadelphia, Pennsylvania

Covered: Harrisburg, Pennsylvania

Light at the End of the Tunnel: Harrisburg, Pennsylvania

Guidance—Bodie Island Lighthouse in Cap Hatteras, North Carolina

Soaring—Bodie Island Lighthouse in Cape Hatteras, North Carolina

**Relaxation in
Kill Devil Hills, NC**

**Home Away from Home in
North Carolina**

Moving Day, Alyssa's Room

Alyssa's Graduation from F.I.U. with a Master of Science in Information Technology

Blue Lagoon in Rekyjavik, Iceland

A Happy Horse in Rekyjavik, Iceland

Even in Iceland ...

Alyssa in Iceland

Horseback in Reykjavik, Iceland

L.I.P. by Rikki

L.I.P. by Rikki, LLC (Lasting Impressions Photography)
Capturing Beauty Through the Eyes of God

For more information or to book Rikki for
Photography Sessions, check out her website!
www.lipbyrikki.com

www.ingramcontent.com/pod-product-compliance
Lightning Source LLC
LaVergne TN
LVHW051600070426
835507LV00021B/2691